GARLAND LIBRARY OF MEDIEVAL LITERATURE
VOL. 94, SERIES A

ADAM DE LA HALLE
LE JEU DE ROBIN ET MARION

The Garland Library
of Medieval Literature

General Editors
James J. Wilhelm, Rutgers University
Lowry Nelson, Jr., Yale University

Literary Advisors
Ingeborg Glier, Yale University
Frede Jensen, University of Colorado
Sidney M. Johnson, Indiana University
William W. Kibler, University of Texas
Norris J. Lacy, Washington University
Fred C. Robinson, Yale University
Aldo Scaglione, New York University

Art Advisor
Elizabeth Parker McLachlan, Rutgers University

Music Advisor
Hendrik van der Werf, Eastman School of Music

ADAM DE LA HALLE
LE JEU DE ROBIN ET MARION

edited and translated by

Shira I. Schwam-Baird

music edited by

Milton G. Scheuermann, Jr.

GARLAND PUBLISHING, Inc.
New York & London / 1994

Library of Congress Cataloging-in-Publication Data

Adam, de La Halle, ca. 1235–ca. 1288.
  [Jeu de Robin et Marion. English]
  Le jeu de Robin et Marion / Adam de la Halle ;
edited and translated by Shira I. Schwam-Baird ; editor
of melodies Milton G. Scheuermann.
      p.   cm. — (Garland library of medieval litera-
ture ; vol. 94A)
  Includes bibliographical references.
  ISBN 0–8153–0756–X (alk. paper)
  1. Pastoral drama, French. 2. Pastourelles.
I. Schwam-Baird, Shira I. II. Scheuermann, Milton G.
III. Title. IV. Series: Garland library of medieval litera-
ture ; v. 94.
PQ1411.A35E5   1994
842′.1—dc20   93-27318
                                                              CIP

Printed on acid-free, 250-year-life paper
Manufactured in the United States of America

For David and Michaël
SSB

For the New Orleans Musica da Camera
and many years of early music-making
MGS

CONTENTS

Preface of the General Editors

The Garland Library of Medieval Literature was established to make available to the general reader modern translations of texts in editions that conform to the highest academic standards. All of the translations are originals, and were created especially for this series. The translations usually attempt to render the foreign works in a natural idiom that remains faithful to the originals, although in certain cases we have published more poetic versions.

The Library is divided into two sections: Series A, texts and translations; and Series B, translations alone. Those volumes containing texts have been prepared after consultation of the major previous editions and manuscripts. The aim in the edition has been to offer a reliable text with a minimum of editorial intervention. Significant variants accompany the original, and important problems are discussed in the Textual Notes. Volumes without texts contain translations based on the most scholarly texts available, which have been updated in terms of recent scholarship.

Most volumes contain Introductions with the following features: (1) a biography of the author or a discussion of the problem of authorship, with any pertinent historical or legendary information; (2) an objective discussion of the literary style of the original, emphasizing any individual features; (3) a consideration of sources for the work and its influence; and (4) a statement of the editorial policy for each edition and translation. There is also a Select Bibliography, which emphasizes recent criticism on the works. Critical writings are often accompanied by brief descriptions of their importance. Selective glossaries, indices, and footnotes are included where appropriate.

The Library covers a broad range of linguistic areas, including all of the major European languages. All of the important literary forms and genres are considered, sometimes in anthologies or selections.

The General Editors hope that these volumes will bring the general reader a closer awareness of a richly diversified area that has for too long been closed to everyone except those with precise academic training, an area that is well worth study and reflection.

James J. Wilhelm
Rutgers University

Lowry Nelson, Jr.
Yale University

LITERARY INTRODUCTION

by Shira Schwam-Baird

Life of the Author

Little is known but much has been conjectured about the life of Adam de la Halle. Many have assumed his work *Le Jeu de la Feuillée* to be autobiographical and deduced from it "facts" about Adam's father, wife, studies, and travels. However, little can be corroborated by the written historical record although some conjectures are more plausible than others.

His date of birth is open to question, and guesses range from 1220 to 1250 in Arras. More recent scholarship tends to fix on a birth date towards the middle of the thirteenth century. His father, known as "Maistre Henri," was probably a cleric and a municipal employee, serving the "échevins" (municipal magistrates). The *Nécrologe de la Confrérie des Jongleurs et des Bourgeois d'Arras*, edited by Berger and our most accurate source of information about Adam and important figures in Arras, notes the death of Adam's father in 1290. A "feme Henri de le Hale" is listed for 1282, a "femme le Boceus" for 1291, and a "Maroie Hale" for 1287, but it is impossible to know if the first refers to Adam's mother or a later wife of Maître Henri, if the second is a second or third wife to the father or possibly Adam's wife, or if the third is Adam's wife or wife of another person with that surname (there are fifteen in the necrology). Adam himself does not figure in the document which supports the argument that he died outside of Arras.

Certain statements and themes treated in Adam's *Jeu de la Feuillée* and *Congés* have led to conjectures that Adam pursued studies at the Vauchelles Abbey, that he was raised or educated under the protection of influential lords named Normant, that he studied or at least desired to study in Paris, that while quite young he married a woman named Maroie, and that due to disturbances in Arras he and his father fled to Douai for a period of time. None of these suppositions can be confirmed and some are rather doubtful (Dufournet, *A la recherche de lui-même* 43-61). However, Adam's service with Robert II, count of Artois, recounted in the anonymous *Jeu du pèlerin*, is much more likely to be true. This short piece precedes the *Jeu de Robin et Marion* in B.N. ms. fr. 25566 and serves as its prologue. A pilgrim tells how Adam was called into the service of the count of Artois, who was impressed with his poetic skills; he implies that Adam followed him to Italy and mentions the Italian cities where he has heard Adam praised. It is known that the count had been sent to Naples to aid his uncle, Charles d'Anjou, in 1282, and Adam's composition of the (short or unfinished) epic, *Le Roi de Sicile*, dedicated to Charles d'Anjou, apparently confirms his own presence there.

The date of Adam's death can be fixed at some time between 1285 and 1289. The *terminus a quo* would have to be the death of Charles d'Anjou, the subject of his *Roi de Sicile*, on January 7, 1285 (Nelson xv). The *terminus ad quem* would be February 2, 1289, the date of a curious explicit to a copy of the *Roman de Troie* (B.N. ms. fr. 375) written by a scribe named Jehan Madot, who claims to be the nephew of "Adans li boçus," who, he says, unfortunately left Arras, where he had been feared and loved ("cremas et amés") and died away from his home (Coussemaker xxvi-xxvii). There has been speculation that Adam lived at least as late as 1306 due to the appearance of the name "Maistre adam le Boscu" in a document attesting to the payment of minstrels hired to perform at the celebration of the dubbing of Prince Edward in Westminster (Faral 95, n. 4; Gégou, "Mort en 1288?" 113-17), but that has been fairly well refuted by Cartier (see bibliography).

Arras in the thirteenth century was home to a prosperous bourgeoisie and an active literary scene. Adam probably composed much of his work (his known output consists of 36 chansons, 17 "jeux-partis," 16 rondeaux, 5 motets, a "congé," *Le Roi de Sicile*, *Le Jeu de la Feuillée*, and *Le Jeu de Robin et Marion* [Nelson xiv]) against a cultural background including a confraternity known as the "Confrérie des Jongleurs et des Bourgeois d'Arras" and a literary competition called the "Puy d'Arras." The confraternity is known from a manuscript which conserves the rules of the organization and the above-mentioned necrology of its members (Paris, B.N. ms. fr. 8541). Also known as "Notre Dame des Ardents," its purpose was "charitable and religious" (Richardson 166). Traditionally the confraternity was the keeper of a miraculous candle that, according to legend, had been bestowed on two intermediary jongleurs to present to the community of Arras in order to cure those suffering from ergotism (known then as "le mal des ardents" or St. Anthony's fire) at the beginning of the twelfth century (Berger 247-48).

All knowledge about the Puy d'Arras comes from references to it in the poetry of various Artesian poets and analogies with the later puys of Amiens and Valenciennes. It was a literary society which apparently held a regular competition in which poets presented their work to be judged. Its origins are unknown, but Richardson speculates that it may have been formed by former jongleur members of the "confrérie" who, in the late twelfth century, were temporarily banished by the aristocratic members, who disliked being associated with lowly poets and performers (164-65).

The connections between the two organizations are unclear. Many jongleurs "whose work indicates that they participated in the 'puy' were also . . . members of the 'Confrérie des Jongleurs et des Bourgeois'"

(Richardson 166). Adam's participation in these societies is unknown for, as stated above, his name does not appear in the confraternity necrology and his poems make no mention that they are intended for presentation at the puy. However, it is likely that he was active in the literary scene for his name appears in poems by his contemporaries. Baude Fastoul, for example, addresses him in his "Congé" as "fil maistre Henri Adan" ("Adam, the son of Master Henry"). In many of his jeux-partis he engages in poetic repartee with the well-known one-time "Prince du Puy," Jehan Bretel, and he satirizes the Puy d'Arras and the patricians of Arras in his *Jeu de la Feuillée*.

Adam's name is variously "Adam de le Hale" (the *le* is a Picardism), "Adam le Bossu," "le Bossu d'Arras," or "Adam d'Arras." "De le Hale" is the surname that appears in certain manuscripts, whereas in others he is "le Bossu" ("the Hunchback"), a sobriquet that was attached to his family and probably not due to any physical handicap of his own (in the necrology his father appears as "Bochu Maistre Henri"). Such descriptive nicknames were common in the Middle Ages and the necrology from Arras gives numerous examples (Cartier 117). In the *Jeu du Pèlerin*, the pilgrim identifies Adam by two of his names: "Maistres Adans li Bochus estoit chi apelés,/ Et la Adans d'Arras" ("Master Adam the Hunchback he was called here,/ And there, Adam of Arras"; vv. 25-26). Once away from Arras, Adam was apparently identified with his place of origin for he calls himself the same in the epic he worked on in Italy, *Le Roi de Sicile*. His sobriquet seems to have bothered him, however, for in that same work he denies being hunchbacked: "On m'apele bochu, mais je ne le sui mie" ("I am called hunchbacked, but I am not so" [my translation]; Coussemaker 285). Perhaps Jehan Bretel was trying to annoy him in the eleventh jeu-parti when he accused Adam of answering him "bochuement" ("awkwardly" or "wrongheadedly" [my translation]; Coussemaker 177).

Dating Adam's work is problematic. His love songs are traditionally attributed to his youth, but nothing can corroborate this assumption. The fifteen jeux-partis in

which Adam debates questions of love with Jehan Bretel had
to have been composed before the death of the latter in
1272. Based on Berger's research in the confraternity
necrology, *Le Jeu de la Feuillée*, which mentions many actual
persons and controversies in Arras, is dated 1276 (Berger,
2nd vol. 106). Adam's *Congé* is widely assumed to have been
composed at the same time, but Dufournet argues for an
earlier date. The *Congé* praises certain rich bourgeois from
whom Adam perhaps hoped to receive support, and he writes
tenderly of an unidentified woman he loves. In *Feuillée*, all
is disillusion and satire, and the woman he desired and
married, now named Maroie, is ugly and constraining. Thus
Dufournet would have *Le Jeu de la Feuillée* a later work of
disillusion (*A la recherche* 50-55). *Le Roi de Sicile* must have
been written some time between Adam's departure for Italy,
probably 1282, when he followed Robert of Artois, and the
death of Charles d'Anjou in 1285.

Most scholars accept the (unprovable) theory that *Le Jeu
de Robin et Marion* was also composed during Adam's stay in
Italy, presumably for the entertainment of homesick troops.
The pilgrim in the prologue to the play, *Le Jeu du Pèlerin*
(*not* composed by Adam), states that the count asked Adam
to write a "dit" to prove his poetic ability, but the name of
the work is not given, nor is there any indication that the
play that follows the prologue is meant to be that work. In
addition, Adam could have entered Robert's service before
he went to Italy, so that even if *Robin et Marion* is the work
mentioned, it might have been written before the departure
for Italy. In his article "Du *Jeu de Robin et Marion* au *Jeu de
la Feuillée*," Dufournet argues against the general tide of
opinion for the thesis that *Robin et Marion* precedes *Feuillée*.
Basing himself solely on literary elements, Dufournet finds
parallels between the two works that indicate the former to
be a first attempt to explore certain themes that receive
greater development in the latter. But Dufournet admits the
impossibility of proving his theory conclusively.

Artistic Achievement

In the nineteenth century Monmerqué and Michel dubbed *Robin et Marion* the first comic opera in French, and it has often been referred to as such ever since. Though it is true that Adam's combination of spoken dialogue with sung portions in a profane setting was innovative, the modern term is a misnomer and an awkward anachronism. The first half of the play is, as has often been noted, a dramatized pastourelle. In the opening scene, Marion sings a known refrain about her sweetheart, Robin. A knight comes along who likewise sings a known refrain, this one typical of opening lines of pastourelle poems. He and Marion engage in a dialogue in which the knight first requests to know why she sings her song, and then asks for information on game birds, since he is out hunting. A series of misunderstandings and puns follows, displaying either Marion's wit or ignorance, and then the conversation turns amorous. The knight invites Marion to go off to "play" with him, but the shepherdess repulses his advances and declares her loyalty to Robin. The knight eventually accepts her refusal and goes off singing another typical pastourelle refrain.

Robin's arrival is accompanied by a duet between him and Marion. Marion informs him of what has happened, reassures him, and they proceed to lunch together. Following that, Robin entertains his sweetheart with a series of acrobatic dance steps, what Guy calls "une rude gymnastique" (519). They decide to extend the party to include their friends and Robin goes off to call them. In the meantime the knight, who is looking for his falcon, comes upon Marion again and resumes his attempt at seduction, which Marion repulses as vehemently as before.

After leaving her, the knight finds Robin mishandling his falcon and strikes him. Her sweetheart's cries bring Marion back on stage where the knight, forgoing any attempt at courtesy, carries Marion off by force. Gautier and Baudon join the lamenting Robin, and the three decide to hide in the bushes to see what the knight will do. As the scene switches to Marion and the knight, we see the former rejecting any gift the latter offers to attempt to win her affections. With a movement of mild disgust ("Certes, voirement sui je beste/ Quant a ceste beste m'areste"; "I must truly be a simpleton/ To have stopped to dally with this creature!" vv. 377-78), the knight releases his prey, and Marion returns to Robin, whom she gently chides for his ineffectual blustering. So ends the first part of the play, very close to the middle verse of the work (v. 411 out of 762 verses).

The second half of the play is a dramatized "bergerie," that genre often considered a sub-genre of the pastourelle, in which a poet-narrator normally recounts coming upon a group of shepherds and shepherdesses and observing their dances, games, disputes, and lovemaking. In *Robin et Marion* the poet-narrator has disappeared, but our rustic group plays games, prepares a picnic, disputes verbally without coming to blows, and finishes with a farandole according to the best bergerie tradition. In the course of this activity, Robin salvages his reputation somewhat by rescuing one of Marion's sheep from a wolf, and soon after Robin and Marion become engaged, if not married, with a pledge and a kiss. (It appears to be a simple pledge to marry, but at least one reader thought it a marriage. A later hand wrote in the title *Mariage de Robin et de Marion* on manuscript *A*.)

Adam's work is most certainly an innovation. First, *Robin et Marion* and *Feuillée* are the first attempts at theater in the French language on a profane subject (Maillard 167). Furthermore, *Robin et Marion* is the first and apparently the only medieval dramatization of the lyric forms pastourelle and bergerie. He alone has fleshed out the stock characters of shepherd, shepherdess, and aristocratic seducer.

Judgments on *Robin et Marion* have ranged from Guy's epithet of "graceful and charming" (531) to Varty's bawdy reading that sees several occurrences of staged copulation ("Le Mariage, la courtoisie et l'ironie comique"). Mazouer finds Marion fresh and naïve, genuinely ignorant about the noble occupation of hunting, (demonstrated by her puzzlement about the falcon's head covering in v. 51), but witty enough to rail the knight over the birds he hunts in vv. 25-46 (380-81). Robin is judged to be "natural" in his rusticity, a "matamore" (braggart without, coward within), an awkward though sincere lover, and never vulgar; peasant vulgarity is left to Gautier (391). Dane develops a theory that Adam's play is a parody of the lyric pastourelle, replete with obscenity and written in a period when literature was increasingly controlled by the bourgeoisie, who had no use for the now meaningless language of the traditional lyric pastourelle (Dane 142).

Brusegan is similarly aware of the erotic and obscene elements in the play which link it to the fabliaux (120), but takes the sociological approach that sees the play as a bourgeois demonstration of the "vilenie" of the peasant class, from which the burgeoning middle class had separated itself (119). The sociological approach however does not jibe with the (albeit unproved) assumption that Adam wrote the play for Robert d'Artois and his knights in Naples (the basis for the 1282 dating), for in such a case the appeal to bourgeois sensibilities would not make sense. Brusegan also stresses the carnival elements in the play, such as the election of a shepherd as king, the dances and the meals (128), points which Dufournet picks up ("Complexité et ambiguïté" 156). Dufournet finds that the misunderstandings between Marion and the knight emphasize the impossibility of communication between these two characters who come from different worlds, and that Adam's work, unlike the lyric pastourelle, is innovative in introducing us to the reality of the peasant world ("Complexité et ambiguïté" 144).

In direct contrast is Axton who argues that far from being a "direct imitation of rustic life," *Robin et Marion* represents the "aristocratic image of idealized country sports" (141), making it an early predecessor of Marie Antoinette's playing at shepherdess. It often seems more likely, though, that Adam's shepherds and shepherdesses are themselves playing at being aristocrats, for they regularly address each other as "biau seigneur" ("fair lord") and use courtly vocabulary, asking Peronnelle, for example, to tell about "the greatest joy that [she] ever had from love" (vv.

556-57). Dufournet sees this as a source of the humor in the play, especially when a "bonne chanson" ("a good song") is Gautier's howling of a line from a scatological mock epic (v. 728; Dufournet ed. 23).

Sources and Influences

The lyric pastourelle and its sub-genre the bergerie, as we have already seen, are the foundation on which Adam built his play. As a genre, it is not always easy to define the boundaries of what is a pastourelle and what is not (Paden ix-xi), and critics differ profoundly on who wrote pastourelles and with what intent. The basic formula is the attempt at seduction on the part of a man, apparently upper class, (usually on horse), of a shepherdess whom he comes upon in a country setting. Almost all critics notice stress on the difference in rank, and the knight of Adam's play takes pains to remind Marion of his social superiority: "Cuideriés empirier de moi,/ Qui si lonc jetés me proiere?/ Chevaliers sui, et vous bregiere ("Would you think yourself worse off with me,/ You who reject so decidedly my entreaty?/ I am a knight and you, a shepherdess," vv. 86-88).

The reason for that stress could be satirical, if pastourelles were written by clerics to demonstrate the brutality and coarse sensuality of knights who demean themselves by consorting with lower class women (Jackson 156). It may be a cover, a disguise by the courtly poet, who would like to rape the lady he worships in the "chanson courtoise," but cannot unless he dresses her in a shepherdess' dress (Gravdal 371-72). Gravdal points out that rape occurs in one-fifth of all extant pastourelles and posits that the genre throughout celebrates that act. Paden counters her argument with the observation that in many of the eighty per cent of the poems where rape does not occur, gifts are involved and prostitution is implicated, which is compatible with the fact that prostitution was often tolerated outside of city walls in the thirteenth century ("Rape in the Pastourelle" 336). Whereas Gravdal focuses on the reality of the sexual violence in the pastourelle poems (citing Andreas

Capellanus' recommendation that a male aristocrat employ force to obtain "love" from a peasant woman if she is not willing to grant her favors), Paden focuses on the fictionality of the characters and events, calling it an "erotic fantasy" (345) and suggesting that Capellanus' advice may simply have been a parody of the pastourelle genre already in existence (347).

In the attention these critics pay to the erotic forcefulness of the poems, whether a rape occurs or not, they draw on the work done by Zink on the pastourelle in which he explores how the pastourelle became the literary expression of sexual desire in the north. The "fin'amors" of the south was adulterous and sexual without guilt, but in the north, courtly love was imposed upon by the church's moral doctrine, which purged it of its sexuality and made it platonic, rendering the courtly songs chaste and ethereal and driving all erotic desire out of the courts and into the countryside. Zink poses the question: why a shepherdess? His answer: she is the human creature closest to nature and to beasts, to creatures without a soul, the mythic lascivious "femme sauvage" who can thus be approached as the object of [male] carnal desire in its purest state (118). We see that Adam's knight refers to Marion as an animal: "Certes, voirement sui je beste/ Quant a ceste beste m'areste!" ("I must truly be a simpleton/ To have stopped to dally with this creature!" vv. 377-78).

There is much that is original, however, in Adam's reworking of the lyric genre. First, there is no rape or successful seduction. Second, rather than be beaten or forced to retire by a group of threatening shepherds armed with clubs (which occurs in many pastourelles), the knight withdraws with his aristocratic dignity intact when he tires of the game of trying to win Marion's favors. And third, the poet-narrator *I* of the pastourelle has disappeared and attention is instead focused on Marion as the central protagonist (Brownlee 430-31). The knight disappears after verse 379, and Marion is the axis of transition between the pastourelle section and the bergerie section. There again, Adam's fleshing out of the peasant characters, with their quarrels and discussions and bawdy jokes, serves to distance the play from its lyric parent, the bergerie, and makes a bow to the developing genre of the fabliaux.

Fourteen per cent of the text of *Robin et Marion* is sung (Maillard 172). However, despite Adam's reputation as a great musician, it is likely that much of the music in this play is not original. Jones sensed that Adam drew on "some ready source" for the songs in his play and presumed it to be popular folk songs of the time (140). Studies by Chailley and Maillard discuss the fact that the sung texts were often known ditties that were inserted in Adam's work as they often were in romances and songs of the time, especially pastourelles and bergeries (Chailley 112). Chailley claims that Adam thus gave to his audience the pleasure of recognizing known melodies that fit the subject of the play (114). For example, the refrain "Hé, resveille toi, Robin/ Car on en maine Marot," ("Hey! wake up, Robin,/ For someone is taking Marion away," v. 341-42), is found in a pastourelle by Huitace de Fontaine (Bartsch III, 13) and in the *Salut d'amour* (Maillard 90). (See musical introduction for further discussion.)

Editorial Policy for This Text and Translation

Robin et Marion survives in three manuscripts: *P* (Paris, B.N. ms. fr. 25566, ff. 39-48^v), *Pa* (Paris, B.N. ms. fr. 1569, ff. 140-144^v), and *A* (Aix-en-Provence, Bibliothèque Méjanes ms. 572, ff. 1-11^v). Both *P* and *A* contain the music for the portions to be sung, whereas the scribe of *Pa* left space for music which was never inserted. *P* has generally been chosen as the base manuscript for previous editions, with the exception of Langlois, and I have found no reason to differ from this practice. Though both *P* and *Pa* date from the late 13th or early 14th century, *P* appears to be closest to what was probably Adam's original language which contained numerous Picard dialectical traits. If *P* and *Pa* are descended from the same copy, as has been posited (Langlois edition, ix), *Pa* is still less usable as a base manuscript as its scribe apparently modified the Picard spelling, and, in addition, the last ten lines of the text are missing. *A* has been ruled out as the best manuscript due to its deteriorated condition which makes certain passages almost impossible to read, and due to the language, clearly Francien, which dates it to the middle or latter 14th century (Varty, *Robin et Marion* 22).

The text has been freshly transcribed from *P* with little editorial emendation except where noted. In a few instances, especially where the interpolations (which occur, like the prologue, *Le Jeu du pèlerin*, only in *P*) caused modification of the text, I have corrected the text from the other manuscripts (see Appendix C for text and translation of the two interpolations). The scribe of *P* had a tendency to misplace rubrics and these have been corrected and noted. However, certain other scribal anomalies, such as variation in the spelling of names (Li chevaliers/ Li chevalies, Peronnele/ Perronele), and inconsistencies in use of the nominal case *s* in the vocative, have been left as is. Diacritical marks have been added following policies outlined in Foulet and Speer's *On Editing Old French Texts*. All scribal abbreviations have been resolved, modern punctuation added, and distinction made between *i* and *j*, and between *u* and *v*. The title comes from the incipit in *P*. All sung portions are in italics.

V·ariants are provided from the other two manuscripts. I have adopted a modified version of Varty's method for recording variants which is much easier to read than traditional arrangements and is suitable to an edition whose text survives in no more than three or four manuscripts. Unlike him, however, I have abbreviated words of more than two letters that do not differ in that verse in order to highlight just what is different in each variant.

The translation of the text is as literal as possible with allowances made for the differences in syntax and idiom between Old French and modern English. Literalness was a goal due to the fact that some performance translations of this play into English exist which take considerable liberties with the original text. Such is the prerogative and proper realm of performance whose duty it is to entertain its audience. However the purpose of this work is to provide a scholarly translation as close to the original as possible which may then serve as the basis for performance adaptations where desired. Therefore no attempt has been made to force the text into rhyming couplets or otherwise transpose what seems awkward due to certain incompatibilities between the two languages. I have, however, attempted to achieve a line-by-line correspondence between text and translation, a task made easier by the non-lyric nature of the text, and have succeeded in most cases.

Names in Old French sometimes differ significantly in spelling in the two-case system (Marion/ Marotain), and in this play in particular, characters are often referred to by diminutives of their names (Marion/ Marote, Marotele; Peronnele/ Perrete, Perrote; Robin/ Robinet). For the translation, I have generally adopted the modern spelling of the non-diminutive name, occasionally expressing the sense of the diminutive, such as affection, by adding a word to the translation; i.e., "dear Robin" for "Robinet." I owe a great debt to previous editors and translators of this delightful text, and though I may have found a few of their mistakes, they helped me find a great many more of my own. My gratitude and appreciation of their excellent work is hereby acknowledged.

Dufournet's edition and French translation of *Robin et Marion* contains extensive notes glossing literary, philological and grammatical aspects of the text. I have made no attempt to reproduce his comprehensive work, but where I deemed it necessary, I have supplemented understanding of the text not sufficient perhaps from the translation alone with explanatory notes. The Select Bibliography indicates sources for further reading and research.

Grateful mention must be made of the New Orleans Musica da Camera whose directors, Milton G. Scheuermann, Jr. and Thaïs St. Julien first got me involved with this text through their lovely production of *Le Jeu de Robin et Marion*. I would also like to express my appreciation to James J. Wilhelm and Hendrik van der Werf for their excellent editorial help in this project.

INTRODUCTION TO THE MUSIC

by Milton G. Scheuermann, Jr.

As mentioned in the Literary Introduction to this volume by Shira Schwam-Baird, two of the manuscript sources of *Le Jeu de Robin et Marion* (*P* and *A*) contain melodies for the songs. Minor differences between the two exist. Since the subject of this volume deals exclusively with an edition and translation of *P*, the transcriptions of the melodies of that source are the ones contained herein. And since the text and a translation of the short *Jeu du Pèlerin* are also included, I have provided transcriptions of the two brief melodies from that play. These two songs are indicated in the transcription as Nos. X1 and X2.

The task of transcribing the music in *P* presents few difficulties since the manuscript is in good physical condition, and note pitches and rhythmic values are fairly well defined. The poor condition of manuscript *A* makes it very difficult, if not impossible, to accurately read and transcribe some of the songs. Some differences between the two, however, can be discerned. Notable are the following: the music and text of Song No. 1 are shorter in *A*. The song is built on the same melodic formula as that in *P* but is not as extended. Song No. 4 has a differently constructed melodic ending to the first line of text in *A* and the second text line has a slightly different melodic curve. Song No. 6 in *A* has shorter music and text for the opening and closing lines. The poor condition of *A* makes it difficult to accurately discern with certainty differences in Song No. 16. It can be seen from the clef, however, that it is notated a fifth lower than that in *P*.

It is not known whether Adam de la Halle composed the songs in *Robin et Marion* or adapted existing simple folk melodies to suit the action of the play. Only in two of the songs does the range exceed the interval of a sixth (Nos. 8 and 16 have a range of an octave and a seventh respectively) and could suggest that they were intended to be sung by untrained voices. The brevity of the pieces also may suggest that they were performed by nonprofessionals. This supports the conjecture that the play was to be performed as a courtly entertainment (this would also support the supposition that it was intended for the court followers of Robert of Artois in Italy rather than common soldiers).

Although Adam's monophonic chansons are in non-mensural notation in their original manuscripts, his three-part rondeaux, and the songs in *Robin et Marion* (both in *P* and *A*) are in typical French mensural notation of the thirteenth century. In the polyphonic rondeaux mensural notation is an aid to the proper vertical alignment of the parts. Some scholars refer to the songs of *Robin et Marion* as both "dance songs" and "refrains." Dance songs were in measured notation (Stevens 186-96) apparently for the purposes of ease of communal dance or singing. It seems unlikely, however, that the majority of these songs would have been performed by more than one person in the context of the play, and only one, No. 10, has text that indicates it really should be danced. This does not preclude the possibility of other songs being danced by individual characters in the play. From a performer's standpoint it could be argued that measured notation would make the songs easier to remember, a feature that would be appreciated by a nonprofessional singer. And memorable music could only be beneficial for a trouvère who depended on his music for his livelihood. If the songs are considered refrains (Gennrich, *Rondeaux* 85-89; van den Boogaard), that is, snippets of well-known text (and possibly music) taken from a pre-existing source and inserted into a new work, this reinforces the appreciation of *Robin et*

Marion as a more courtly than popular entertainment, as the use of refrain was part of the courtly tradition in music and poetry. Song No. 15 (*Audigier*) stands alone as one of only two surviving examples of a melodic formula used in the epic poetry type, the *chanson de geste*.

Music for No. 3B is not contained in the manuscript but the text suggests that it is the same as 3A. Similarly, complete music for No. 14B is not contained in the manuscript but has been added in the transcription to match that of No. 14A. The part not notated in the manuscript has been enclosed, in keeping with standard practice, within brackets.

The characters in *Robin et Marion* were archetypal in the pastourelles of the period and found their way into other musical texts. Indeed, there exist some fifty or so thirteenth century motets whose texts deal with these personalities and the themes of love and seduction in a pastourelle setting. Most of these so-called "Robin motets" are found in the major manuscript sources of the twelfth and thirteenth centuries (Bamberg, Staatliche Bibliothek, Lit. 115; Montpellier, Faculté de Médecine, H196; and Wolfenbüttel, Herzog-August Bibliothek, Helmstedt 1099 [or 1206]). Two of these motets include melodies and texts contained in the play. *Mout me fu gries / Robins m'aimme / Portare*, in both the Bamberg and Montpellier manuscripts, uses No. 1 (*Robin m'aime*), with music and text slightly altered, as the duplum, and *En Mai / L'autre jour / Hé, resvelle toi*, in the Montpellier manuscript, has the complete melody and opening line of the text of No. 12 (*Hé, resveille toi*) as the tenor line. The melody without text of No. 12 is also found, although slightly altered and extended, in the fourteenth century Ivrea manuscript (Biblioteca Capitolare) as the tenor line of the two-part virelai, *Prenés l'abre / [Hé, resvelle toi]*.

I would like to thank Professor Hendrik van der Werf for kindly reviewing these transcriptions and offering well-taken advice. My appreciation is also extended to my co-director of the New Orleans Musica da Camera, Thaïs St. Julien, for her input, helpful suggestions and editorial assistance.

SELECT BIBLIOGRAPHY

I. Major Editions

Bartsch, Karl Friedrich and Adolf Horning. *La Langue et la littérature françaises depuis le IXe siècle jusqu'au XIVe siècle*. Paris: Maisonneuve & Ch. Leclerc, 1887. 523-48. Text based on *P* with variants from *Pa*.

Coussemaker, E. de. *Oeuvres complètes d'Adam de la Halle*. Paris, 1872; rpt. Geneva: Slatkine Reprints, 1970. 347-412. Text and music; based on *P* with variants from *A*.

D'Aussy, Legrand. *Fabliaux ou contes, fables et romans du XIIe et du XIIIe siècle*. 3e éd. Tome 2. Paris: Jules Renouard, 1829. Appendice 1-15. Text from *P*.

Douhet, Jules de (Comte). *Dictionnaire des mystères*. Paris-Petit-Montrouge: J.-P.Migne, 1854; rpt. Geneva: Slatkine Reprints, 1977. 1455-1522. Text and modern French translation; based on *P*.

Dufournet, Jean. *Le Jeu de Robin et de Marion*. Paris: Flammarion, 1989. Text, translation into modern French and extensive notes; based on *P*.

Gennrich, Friedrich. *Le Jeu de Robin et de Marion: Li Rondel Adam*. Langen Bei Frankfurt am Main, 1962. Text based on Langlois edition, and music.

Langlois, Ernest. *Le Jeu de Robin et Marion: suivi du Jeu du pèlerin*. Paris: Champion, 1924. Attempt at reconstruction of original text and original Picard dialect; based on all three manuscripts, with variants.

Monmerqué, Louis J.N. et Francisque Michel. *Théâtre français au Moyen Âge*. Paris: Firmin-Didot, 1929. Text and modern French translation; based on *P*.

Pauphilet, Albert. *Jeux et sapiences du Moyen Âge*. Paris: Gallimard (Bibliothèque de la Pléiade), 1951. 159-202. Composite of three manuscripts and previous editions.

Rambeau, A. *Die dem trouvère Adam de la Hale zugeschriebenen Dramen. Ausgaben und Abhandlungen aus dem Gebiete der Romanischen Philologie* 58. Marburg: N.G. Elwert'sche, 1886. 12-70. Diplomatic edition of all three manuscripts.

Varty, Kenneth. *Le Jeu de Robin et de Marion*. London: Harrap, 1960. Text based on *P* with variants.

II. Translations

Axton, Richard and John Stevens. *Medieval French Plays*. Oxford: Basil Blackwell, 1971. Modern English translation for performance.

Beck, Jean and J. Murray Gibbon. *The Play of Robin and Marion: Mediaeval Folk Comedy in One Act*. Boston: C.C. Birchard & Co., 1928. Modern English rhymed translation for performance; revised and abridged version of original old French text.

Brasseur-Péry, Annette. *Adam le Bossu: Le Jeu de Robin et Marion*. Paris: Champion, 1970. Modern French translation of Langlois edition.

Cohen, Gustave. *Le Jeu de Robin et Marion.* Paris: Delagrave, 1935. Modern French rhymed translation with music transcribed by Jacques Chailley; abridged text.

Langlois, Ernest. *Le Jeu de la Feuillée et Le Jeu de Robin et Marion.* Paris: Boccard, 1923. Modern French translation.

Milhaud, Darius, dir. *The Play of Robin and Marion: Dances and Songs after Adam de la Halle: English version freely adapted from the Old French by Roger Maren: Vocal score.* New York: Edward B. Marks Music Corp., 1951. Modern English rhymed adaptation for performance commissioned by the Julliard Opera Theater.

III. Criticism and Study Guides

Axton, Richard. *European Drama of the Early Middle Ages.* London: Hutchinson & Co., Ltd., 1974.

Bartsch, Karl, ed. *Altfranzösische romanzen und pastourellen.* 1870. Darmstadt: Wissenschaftliche Buchgesellschaft, 1967.

Bastin, Julia. "Compte-rendu de la *Lexique des oeuvres d'Adam de la Halle de Gilbert Mayer.*" *Romania* 67 (1942-43): 383-97. Corrects and amends Mayer's work.

Berger, Roger. *Le Nécrologe de la Confrérie des Jongleurs et des Bourgeois d'Arras.* 2 vols. Arras, 1963-1970.

Boogaard, N.H.J. van der. *Rondeaux et refrains du XIIe au début du XIVe siècle.* Paris: Klincksieck, 1969.

Brownlee, Kevin. "Transformations of the Couple: Genre and Language in the *Jeu de Robin et Marion.*" *French Forum* 14 (1989): 419-33.

Brusegan, Rosanna. "*Le Jeu de Robin et Marion* et l'ambiguïté du symbolisme champêtre." *The Theatre in* the *Middle Ages*. Herman Braet et al, eds. Leuven: Leuven University Press, 1985. 119-29.

Cartier, Normand R. "La Mort d'Adam le Bossu." *Romania* 89 (1968): 116-24.

Chailley, Jacques. "Adam de la Halle musicien." *Dictionnaire des lettres françaises: Le Moyen Âge*. Paris: Fayard, 1964. 28.

——. "La Nature musicale du *Jeu de Robin et Marion*." *Mélanges d'histoire du théâtre du Moyen Âge et de la Renaissance offerts à Gustave Cohen*. Paris: Nizet, 1950. 111-17.

Dane, Joseph A. "Parody and Satire in Thirteenth-Century Arras." *Studies in Philology* 81 (1984): 1-27; 119-44.

Dufournet, Jean. *Adam de la Halle à la recherche de lui-même ou le Jeu dramatique de la Feuillée*. Paris: SEDES, 1974.

——. Complexité et ambiguïté du *Jeu de Robin et Marion*: L'ouverture de la pièce et le portrait des paysans." *Etudes de philologie romane et d'histoire littéraire offertes à Jules Horrent*. Liège: 1980. 141-59.

——. "Du *Jeu de Robin et Marion* au *Jeu de la Feuillée*." *Etudes de langues et de littérature du Moyen Age offertes à Félix Lecoy*. Paris: Champion, 1973. 73-94.

Faral, Edmond. *Les Jongleurs en France au Moyen Age*. Paris: Champion, 1971.

Gégou, Fabienne. "Adam le Bossu était-il mort en 1288?" *Romania* 86 (1965): 111-17.

——. "La Langue du poète Adam de la Halle dans ses chansons courtoises." *Mélanges de philologie et de littérature romanes offerts à Jeanne Wathelet-Willem.* Liège: Marche Romane, 1978. 175-88.

Gennrich, Friedrich. *Rondeaux, Virelais und Balladen aus dem Ende des XII, dem XIII und dem ersten Drittel des XIV Jahrhunderts*. Göttingen: Max Niemeyer, 1927.

Gossen, Charles T. *Grammaire de l'ancien picard*. Paris: Klincksieck, 1970.

Gravdal, Kathryn. "Camouflaging Rape: The Rhetoric of Sexual Violence in the Medieval Pastourelle." *Romanic Review* 76 (1985): 361-73.

Guy, Henry. *Essai sur la vie et les oeuvres littéraires du trouvère Adan de le Hale*. Paris: Hachette, 1898.

Hard af Segerstad, Kerstin. "Saint Coisne." *Revue de dialectologie romane* 2 (1910): 373-74.

Henry, Albert. "Sur deux passages du *Jeu de Robin et Marion*." *Romania* 73 (1952): 234-38.

Huot, Sylvia. "Transformations of Lyric Voice in the Songs, Motets, and Plays of Adam de la Halle." *Romanic Review* 78 (1987): 148-64.

Jackson, William T.H. "The Medieval Pastourelle as a Satirical Genre." *Philological Quarterly* 31 (1952): 156-70.

Jones, W. Powell. "The Medieval Pastourelle and French Folk Drama." *Harvard Studies and Notes in Philology and Literature* 13 (1931): 129-63.

Langlois, Ernest. "Interpolations du *Jeu de Robin et Marion*." *Romania* 24 (1895): 437-46.

——. "Le Jeu du Roi qui ne ment et le jeu du Roi et de la Reine." *Mélanges Chabaneau: Volume offert à Camille Chabaneau. Romanische Forschungen* 23 (1907): 163-73.

Maillard, Jean. *Adam de la Halle: Perspective musicale*. Paris: Champion, 1982.

Mayer, Gilbert. *Lexique des oeuvres d'Adam de la Halle.* Paris: Droz, 1940.

Mazouer, Charles. "Naïveté et naturel dans le *Jeu de Robin et Marion.*" *Romania* 93 (1972): 378-93.

Ménard, Philippe. "Le Sens du *Jeu de la Feuillée.*" *Travaux de linguistique et de littérature* 16.1 (1978): 381-93.

Paden, William, ed. and trans. *The Medieval Pastourelle.* 2 vols. New York: Garland, 1987.

——. "Rape in the Pastourelle." *Romanic Review* 80 (1989): 331-49.

Richardson, Louise Barbara. "The *Confrérie des Jongleurs et des Bourgeois* and the *Puy d'Arras* in Twelfth and Thirteenth Century Literature." *Studies in Honor of Mario A. Pei.* Chapel Hill: University of North Carolina Press, 1972. 161-71.

Stevens, John. *Words and Music in the Middle Ages.* Cambridge: Cambridge University Press, 1986.

Varty, Kenneth. "Le Mariage, la courtoisie et l'ironie comique dans *Le Jeu de Robin et de Marion.*" *Mélanges de langue et littérature françaises du Moyen Âge et de la Renaissance offerts à Charles Foulon.* Vol. 2. *Marche Romane* 30, 1980. 287-92.

Zink, Michel. *La Pastourelle: Poésie et folklore au Moyen Âge.* Paris: Bordas, 1972.

Adam de la Halle
Le Jeu de Robin et Marion

CHARACTERS

MARION, a young shepherdess, Robin's sweetheart
ROBIN, a young peasant, Marion's sweetheart
THE KNIGHT
GAUTIER BIGHEAD,[1] a young peasant, Robin's cousin
BAUDON, a young peasant, Robin's cousin
HUART, a young peasant, Robin's friend
PERONNELLE, a young shepherdess, Marion's friend
TWO HORN PLAYERS

Chi commenche le gieus de Robin et de Marion c'Adans fist

MARIONS:

> *Robins m'aime, Robins m'a,*
> *Robins m'a demandee, si m'ara.*
> *Robins m'acata cotele*
> *D'escarlate bonne et bele,*   4
> *Souskanie et chainturele,*
>   *A leur i va.*
> *Robins m'aime, Robins m'a,*
> *Robins m'a demandee, si m'ara.*   8

LI CHEVALIERS:

> *Je me repairoie du tournoiement,*
> *Si trouvai Marote seulete au cors gent.*

MARIONS:

> *Hé, Robin, se tu m'aimes,*
> *Par amours, maine m'ent.*[2]   12

LI CHEVALIERS:

> Bergiere, Diex vous doinst bon jour!

MARIONS:

> Diex vous gart, sire!

LI CHEVALIERS:

>   Par amour,
> Douche puchele, or me contés
> Pour coi ceste canchon cantés   16
> Si volentiers et si souvent ——
> *Hé, Robin, se tu m'aimes,*
> *Par amours, maine m'ent?*

MARIONS:

> Biaus sire, il i a bien pour coi;   20
> J'aim bien Robinet, et il moi;
> Et bien m'a moustré qu'il m'a chiere.
> Donné m'a ceste panetiere,
> Ceste houlete et cest coutel.   24

4

Here begins the play of Robin and Marion that Adam made

MARION:
Robin loves me, Robin has me;
Robin asked for me, and will have me.
Robin bought me a dress
Of good cloth, fine and fair,   4
A long gown and a little belt,
  *A leur i va!*³
Robin loves me, Robin has me,
*Robin asked for me and will have me.*⁴   8

THE KNIGHT:
I was returning from the tournament,
And I found lovely Marion all alone.

MARION:
Hey, Robin, if you love me,
I pray you, take me away.   12

THE KNIGHT:
Shepherdess, God give you good day!

MARION:
God keep you, sir!

THE KNIGHT:
                    I pray you,
Sweet girl, now tell me
Why you sing this song   16
So readily and so often ——
Hey, Robin, if you love me
I pray you, take me away?

MARION:
Fair sir, there is good reason;   20
For I love Robin, and he loves me,
And well has he shown me that he holds me dear.
He has given me this satchel,
This shepherd's crook and this knife.   24

5

LI CHEVALIERS:
   Di moi, veïs tu nul oisel
   Voler par deseure les cans?

MARIONS:
   Sire, j'en ai veü, ne sai kans.⁵
   Encore i a en ces buissons   28
   Cardonnereul[e]s et pinçons
   Qui mout cantent joliement.

LI CHEVALIES:
   Si m'aït Dieus, bele au cors gent,
   Che n'est point che que je demant.   32
   Mais veïs tu par chi devant
   Vers ceste riviere nul ane?

MARIONS:
   C'est une beste qui recane?
   J'en vi ier .iii. seur che quemin,   36
   Tous quarchiés aler au molin.
   Est che chou que vous demandés?

LI CHEVALIES:
   Or suis je mout bien assenés!
   Di moi, veïs tu nul hairon?   40

MARIONS:
   Hairons,⁶ sire, par me foi, non;
   Je n'en vi nes un puis quaresme,
   Que j'en vi mengier chiés Dame Eme,
   Me taiien, cui sont ches brebis.   44

LI CHEVALIERS:
   Par foi, or sui jou esbaubis;
   N'ainc mais je ne fui si gabés!

MARIONS:
   Sire, foi que vous mi devés,
   Quele beste est che seur vo main?   48

THE KNIGHT:
    Tell me, have you seen any birds
    Flying over the fields?

MARION:
    I have seen some, I don't know how many sir.
    There are still in these bushes   28
    Some goldfinches and finches
    That sing quite merrily.[7]

THE KNIGHT:
    God help me, fair one,
    That is not at all what I am asking.   32
    Instead, have you seen any ducks
    Anywhere around here, near the river?

MARION:
    You mean a beast that brays?[8]
    Yesterday I saw three on this road,   36
    All loaded to go to the mill.
    Is that what you are asking?

THE KNIGHT:
    Now I am very well informed!
    Tell me: have you seen any herons?   40

MARION:
    Herrings, sir?[9] By my faith, no;
    I haven't seen a one since Lent,
    When I saw some eaten at Dame Emme's,
    My grandmother, whose sheep these are.   44

THE KNIGHT:
    By faith, now I am confounded;
    Never have I been so well mocked!

MARION:
    Sir, in good faith,
    What creature is that on your hand?   48

LI CHEVALIERS:
C'est uns faucons.

MARIONS:

                Mengüe il pain?

LI CHEVALIERS:
Non, mais bonne char.

MARIONS:

                Cele beste?
Esgar! Ele a de cuir le teste![10]
Et ou alés vous?

LI CHEVALIERS:

                En riviere.   52

MARIONS:
Robins n'est pas de tel maniere;
En lui a trop plus de deduit.
A no vile esmuet tout le bruit
Quant il joue de se musete.   56

LI CHEVALIERS:
Or dites, douche bregerete,[11]
Ameriés vous un chevalier?

MARIONS:
Biaus sire, traiiés vous arrier!
Je ne sai que chevalier sont.   60
Deseur tous les homes du mont
Je n'ameroie que Robin.
Chi vient au vespre et au matin,
A moi toudis et par usage.   64
Chi m'aporte de son froumage;
Encore en ai je en mon sain
Et une grant pieche de pain
Que il m'aporta a prangiere.   68

THE KNIGHT:
    It is a falcon.

MARION:
                Does it eat bread?

THE KNIGHT:
    No, it eats good meat.

MARION:
                That creature?
    Look! It has leather on its head!
    Where are you going?

THE KNIGHT:
                Along the riverbank.   52

MARION:
    Robin is so different;
    He's a lot more fun.
    In our village he raises a racket
    When he plays his musette.[12]   56

THE KNIGHT:
    Now tell me, sweet shepherdess,
    Could you love a knight?

MARION:
    Step back, fair sir!
    I don't know what knights are.   60
    Of all the men in the world
    I could love only Robin.
    He comes to see me every day,
    Morning and evening as is his custom,   64
    And brings me some of his cheese;
    I still have some in my bodice[13]
    With a big piece of bread
    That he brought me for lunch.   68

LI CHEVALIERS:
Or me dites, douche bregiere,
Vauriés vous venir avoec moi
Jeuer seur che bel palefroi
Selonc che bosket, en che val?   72

MARIONS AU CHEVALIER:
Aimi! Sire, ostés vo cheval!
A poi que il ne m'a blechie.
Li Robins ne regiete mie
Quant je vois apres se karue.   76

LI CHEVALIERS:
Bregiere, devenés ma drue,
Et faites che que je vous proi.

MARIONS AU CHEVALIER:
Sire, traiés ensus de moi:
Chi estre point ne vous affiert.   80
A poi vos chevaus ne me fiert.
Comment vous apele on?

LI CHEVALIERS:
                              Aubert.

MARIONS AU CHEVALIER:
Vous perdés vo paine, sire Aubert.
Je n'amerai autrui que Robert.   84

LI CHEVALIERS:
Nan, bregiere?

MARIONS AU CHEVALIER:
                    Nan, par ma foi!

LI CHEVALIERS:
Cuideriés empirier de moi,
Qui si lonc jetés me proiere?
Chevaliers sui et vous bregiere.   88

THE KNIGHT:
   Now tell me, sweet shepherdess,
   Would you like to come with me
   To play upon this handsome palfrey
   Along the grove, in that valley there?   72

MARION TO THE KNIGHT:
   Ai! Sir, take away your horse!
   He almost hurt me.
   Robin's horse doesn't kick a bit
   When I walk behind his plow.   76

THE KNIGHT:
   Shepherdess, become my mistress,
   And do what I entreat of you.

MARION TO THE KNIGHT:
   Sir, draw away from me:
   It does not befit you to be here.   80
   Your horse is likely to strike me.
   What is your name?

THE KNIGHT:
                     Aubert.

MARION TO THE KNIGHT:
   You are wasting your time, Sir Aubert.
   I will never love anyone but my Robin.   84

THE KNIGHT:
   No, shepherdess?

MARION TO THE KNIGHT:
                     No, by my faith!

THE KNIGHT:
   Would you think yourself worse off with me,
   You who reject so decidedly my entreaty?
   I am a knight and you, a shepherdess.   88

MARIONS AU CHEVALIER:
>Ja pour che ne vous amerai.
>*Bergeronnete sui mais j'ai*
>*Ami bel et cointe et gai.*

LI CHEVALIERS:
>Bregiere, Diex vous en doinst joie!   92
>Puis qu'ensi est, g'irai me voie.
>Hui mais ne vous sonnerai mot.

MARIONS AU CHEVALIER:
>*Trairi deluriau deluriau deluriele,*
>*Trairi deluriau delur[i]au delurot.*   96

LI CHEVALIERS:
>*Hui main jou chevauchoie lés l'oriere d'un bois;*
>*Trouvai gentil bergiere, tant bele ne vit roys.*
>*Hé! Trairi deluriau deluriau deluriele,*
>*Trairi deluriau deluriau delurot.*   100

MARIONS:
>*Hé! Robechon, leure[14] leure va,*
>*Car vien a moi, leure leure va,*
>*S'irons jeuer, dou leure leure va,*
>*Dou leure leure va.*   104

ROBIN:[15]
>*Hé! Marion, leure leure va,*
>*Je vois a toi, leure leure va,*
>*S'irons jeuer, dou leure leure va,*
>*Dou leure leure va.*   108

MARIONS:
>Robin!

ROBINS:[16]
>   Marote!

MARIONS:
>   Dont viens tu?

MARION TO THE KNIGHT:
    Never for that will I love you.
    A little shepherdess am I, but I have
    A sweetheart handsome, graceful and gay.

THE KNIGHT:
    Shepherdess, may God give you joy of him!   92
    Since it is so, I will go my way.
    Henceforth I won't say another word to you.

MARION TO THE KNIGHT:
    Trairi deluriau deluriau deluriele,
    Trairi deluriau deluriau delurot.[17]   96

THE KNIGHT:
    This morning I was riding along the edge of a wood;
    Found a pretty shepherdess, so lovely no king ever saw.
    Hey! Trairi deluriau deluriau deluriele
    Trairi deluriau deluriau delurot.   100

MARION:
    Hey! Robin, leure leure va,[18]
    Come to me, leure leure va,
    And we'll go play, dou leure leure va,
    Dou leure leure va.   104

ROBIN:
    Hey! Marion, leure leure va,
    I come to you, leure leure va,
    And we'll go play, dou leure leure va,
    Dou leure leure va.   108

MARION:
    Robin!

ROBIN:
            Marion!

MARION:
                  Where are you coming from?

ROBINS:
>   Par le saint [Dieu], j'ai desvestu,
>   Pour che qu'i fait froit, men jupel,
>   S'ai pris me cote de burel;   112
>   Et si t'aport des pommes. Tien!

MARIONS:
>   Robin, je te connuc trop bien
>   Au canter si con tu venoies.
>   Et tu ne me reconnissoies?   116

ROBINS:
>   Si fis, au chant et as brebis.

MARIONS:
>   Robin, tu ne sés, dous amis ——[19]
>   Et si ne le tien mie a mal——
>   Par chi vint .i. hom a cheval   120
>   Qui avoit cauchie une moufle,
>   Et portoit aussi c'un escoufle
>   Seur sen poing; et trop me pria
>   D'amer, mais poi i conquesta,   124
>   Car je ne te ferai nul tort.

ROBINS A MAROTE:
>   Marote, tu m'aroies mort.
>   Mais se g'i fusse a tans venus,
>   Ne jou, ne Gautiers li Testus,   128
>   Ne Baudons, mes cousins germains,
>   Diable i eüssent mis les mains,
>   Ja n'en fust partis sans bataille.

MARIONS A ROBIN:
>   Robin, dous amis, ne te caille;   132
>   Mais or faisons feste de nous.

ROBINS:
>   Serai je drois ou a genous?

ROBIN:

> By holy God,[20] because it's cold,
> I took off my cape
> And got my woolen tunic;   112
> And I've brought you some apples. Here!

MARION:

> Robin, I recognized you well
> By your singing as you were coming.
> Didn't you recognize me?   116

ROBIN:

> Of course I did, by the song and by the sheep.

MARION:

> Robin, you're not aware, sweetheart - —
> And don't take it wrong-—
> A man on a horse was here   120
> Who was wearing a mitten,
> And also carried something like a kite-bird[21]
> On his fist; much did he entreat me
> To love him, but little did he achieve,   124
> For I will never do you wrong.

ROBIN TO MARION:

> Marion, you would have killed me.
> But if I had come in time,
> Either I or Gautier Bighead,   128
> Or Baudon, my first cousin,
> Had the devils been with him,
> Never would he have gotten away without a fight.

MARION TO ROBIN:

> Robin, sweetheart, it doesn't matter;   132
> Let's just enjoy ourselves.

ROBIN:

> Shall I stand or kneel?

MARIONS:
    Vien si te sié encoste moi,
    Si mengerons.

ROBINS:
                  Et jou l'otroi;   136
    Je serai chi, lés ton costé.
    Mais je ne t'ai riens aporté;
    Si ai fait certes grant outrage.

MARIONS:
    Ne t'en caut, Robin, encore ai je   140
    Du froumage chi en mon sain,
    Et une grant pieche de pain,
    Et des poumes que m'aportas.

ROBINS:
    Diex, que chis froumages est cras!   144
    Ma seur, mengüe.

MARIONS:
                  Et tu aussi.
    Quant tu vieus boire, si le di:
    Vés chi fontaine en .i. pochon.

ROBINS:
    Diex, qui ore eüst du bacon   148
    Te taiien, bien venist a point!

MARIONS:
    Robinet, nous n'en arons point,
    Car trop haut pent as quieverons.
    Faisons de che que nous avons;   152
    Ch'est assés pour le matinee.

ROBINS:
    Diex, que j'ai le panche lassee
    De le choule de l'autre fois!

MARION:
> Come sit here next to me,
> And we shall eat.

ROBIN:
>   All right then;   136
> I will be here by your side.
> But I haven't brought you anything;
> I have surely committed a great offense.

MARION:
> It doesn't matter, Robin, I still have   140
> Some cheese here in my bodice,
> And a big piece of bread,
> And the apples you brought me.

ROBIN:
> My God, how rich this cheese is!   144
> Eat some, my dear.

MARION:
>   And you too.
> When you want to drink, just say so:
> Here is some water in a jug.

ROBIN:
> Lord, how good it would be to have   148
> Some of your gramma's bacon right now!

MARION:
> Dear Robin, we won't have any,
> For it's hung high on the rafters.
> Let us make do with what we have;   152
> It is enough for the morning.

ROBIN:
> Heavens, how sore my belly is
> From lacrosse the other day!

MARIONS:
   Di, Robin, foy que tu mi dois,   156
   Choulas tu? Que Diex le te mire!

ROBINS:
   Vous l'orrés bien dire,
   Bele, vous l'orrés bien dire.

MARIONS:
   Di, Robin, veus tu plus mengier?   160

ROBINS:
   Naie, voir.

MARIONS:
               Dont metrai je arrier
   Che pain, che froumage en mon sain
   Dusqu'a ja que nous arons fain.

ROBINS:
   Ains le met en te panetiere!   164

MARIONS:
   Et vés li chi. Robin, quel chiere!
   Proie et commande, je ferai.

ROBINS:
   Marote, et jou esprouverai
   Se tu m'ies loiaus amiete,   168
   Car tu m'as trouvé amiet.
   Bergeronnete, douche baisselete,
   Donnés le moi, vostre chapelet,
   Donnés le moi, vostre chapelet.   172

MARIONS:
   Robin, veus tu que je le meche
   Seur ton chief par amourete?

ROBINS:
   Oïl, et vous serés m'amiete;

MARION:
> Say, Robin, on your honor,   156
> Did you play lacrosse? Heaven reward you for it!²²

ROBIN:
> *So you will hear it said,*
> *Fair one, so you will hear it said.*

MARION:
> Say, Robin, do you want any more to eat?   160

ROBIN:
> No, not really.

MARION:
>   Then I will put away
> This bread and cheese in my bodice
> Until we get hungry.

ROBIN:
> Put it in your basket instead!   164

MARION:
> There, it's done. Robin, what a face!
> Entreat and command, I will obey.

ROBIN:
> Dear Marion, I am going to test
> Whether you are my faithful sweetheart true,   168
> For you have found me your lover true.
> *Little shepherdess, sweet little girl,*
> *Give me your garland of flowers,*
> *Give me your garland of flowers.*   172

MARION:
> *Robin, do you want me to put it*
> *On your head as a token of love?*

ROBIN:
> *Yes, and you will be my sweetheart;*

Vous averés ma chainturete, 176
M'aumosniere et mon fremalet.
Bergeronnete, douche baisselete,
Donnés le moi, vostre chapelet.

MARIONS:
Volentiers, men douc amiet. 180
Robin, fai nous .i. poi de feste.

ROBINS:
Veus tu des bras ou de le teste?
Je te di que je sai tout faire.
Ne l'as tu point oï retraire? 184

MARIONS:
Robin, par l'ame ten pere,
Sés tu bien aler du piet?

ROBINS:
Oïl, par l'ame me mere.
Resgarde comme il me siet: 188
Avant et arriere,
Bele, avant et arriere.

MARIONS:
Robin, par l'ame ten pere,
Car nous fai le tour dou chief. 192

ROBINS:
Marot, par l'ame me mere,
J'en venrai mout bien a chief.
I fait on tel chiere,
Bele, i fait on tel chiere? 196

MARIONS:
Robin, par l'ame ten pere,
Car nous fai le tour des bras.

ROBINS:
Marot, par l'ame me mere,

You will have my little belt,   176
My purse and my buckle.
Little shepherdess, sweet little girl,
Give me your garland of flowers.

MARION:

Willingly, my lover sweet.   180
Robin, entertain us a bit.

ROBIN:

Do you want the arm step or the head step?[23]
I tell you I can do everything.
Haven't you heard it told?   184

MARION:

Robin, upon your father's soul,
Can you do the foot step well?

ROBIN:

Yes, upon my mother's soul.
Watch how it becomes me   188
Forwards and backwards,
Fair one, forwards and backwards.

MARION:

Robin, upon your father's soul,
Do for us the head step.   192

ROBIN:

Marion, upon my mother's soul,
I will manage it very well.
Do others look so good at it,
Fair one, do others look so good at it?   196

MARION:

Robin, upon your father's soul,
Do for us the arm step.

ROBIN:

Marion, upon my mother's soul,

Tout ensi con tu vaurras.   200
Est chou la maniere,
Bele, est chou la maniere?

MARIONS:
Robin, par l'ame ten pere,
Sés tu baler au seriaus?[24]   204

ROBINS:
Oïl, par l'ame me mere,
Mais j'ai trop mains de chaviaus
Devant que derriere,
Bele, devant que derriere.   208

MARIONS:
Robin, sés tu mener le treske?

ROBINS:
Oïl, mais li voie est trop freske,
Et mi housel sont desquiré.

MARIONS:
Nous sommes trop bien atiré.   212
Ne t'en caut; or fai, par amour.

ROBINS:
Aten, g'irai pour le tabour
Et pour le muse au grant bourdon.
Et si amenrai chi Baudon,   216
Se trouver le puis, et Gautier.
Aussi m'aront il bien mestier
Se li chevaliers revenoit.

MARIONS:
Robin, revien a grant esploit;   220
Et se tu trueves Peronnele,
Me compaignesse, si l'apele.
Le compaignie en vaura miex.
Ele est derriere ces courtiex   224
Si c'on va au molin Rogier.

Everything just as you like. 200
Is this the way,
Fair one, is this the way?

MARION:
Robin, upon your father's soul,
Can you dance "aux seriaux"?[25] 204

ROBIN:
Yes, upon my mother's soul,
But I have much less hair
In front than behind,
Fair one, in front than behind. 208

MARION:
Robin, can you lead the farandole?

ROBIN:
Yes, but the path is too wet,
And my boots are torn.

MARION:
But we are quite suitably dressed. 212
Don't worry about that; do it, I pray you.

ROBIN:
Wait, I'll go get my drum
And my musette with the big reed-pipe.
And I'll bring Baudon here, 216
If I can find him, and Gautier.
They would also be useful to me
If the knight returned.

MARION:
Robin, come back at full speed; 220
And if you find Peronnelle,
My companion, call her too.
The party will be the better for it.
She is behind those fields 224
On the way to Rogier's mill.

Or te haste!

ROBINS:

Lais me escourchier.
Je ne ferai fors courre.

MARIONS:

Or va!

ROBINS:

Gautiers, Baudon, estes vous la?   228
Ouvrés moi tost l'uis, biau cousin!

GAUTIERS:

Bien soies tu venus, Robin.
C'as tu qui ies si essouflés?

ROBINS:

Que j'ai? Las! Je sui si lassés   232
Que je ne puis m'alaine avoir.

BAUDONS:

Di s'on t'a batu.

ROBINS:

Nenil, voir.

GAUTIERS:

Di tost s'on t'a fait nul despit.

ROBINS:

Signeur, escoutés un petit.   236
Je sui chi venus pour vous deus,
Car je ne sai ques menestreus
A cheval pria d'amer ore
Marotain; si me douch encore   240
Que il ne reviegne par la.

GAUTIERS:

S'il revient, il le comperra!

Now go quickly!

ROBIN:

Let me tuck up my pants.
I'll run the whole way.

MARION:

Now go!

ROBIN:

Gautier, Baudon, are you there?   228
Open the door quickly, dear cousins.

GAUTIER:

Welcome, Robin.
What is the matter, that you are so out of breath?

ROBIN:

What's the matter? Alas! I am so weary   232
That I can't catch my breath.

BAUDON:

Tell us if someone has hit you.

ROBIN:

Indeed not.

GAUTIER:

Say quickly if anyone has done you any injury.

ROBIN:

Gentlemen, listen a bit.[26]   236
I have come here to get you two,
Because some rotten fellow[27]
On a horse made advances just now
To my Marion; and I fear yet   240
That he may return there.

GAUTIER:

If he comes, he will pay for it!

BAUDONS:
Che f[e]ra mon, par ceste teste!

ROBINS:
Vous averés trop bonne feste,   244
Biau seigneur, se vous i venés,
Car vous et Huars i serés,
Et Peronnele. Sont chou gent?
Et s'averés pain de fourment,   248
Bon froumage et clere fontaine.

BAUDONS:
Hé, biau cousin, car nous i maine!

ROBINS:
Mais vous deus irés chele part,
Et je m'en irai pour Huart   252
Et Peronnele.

BAUDONS:
                    Va don, va!

GAUTIERS:
Et nous en irons par deça
Vers le voie devers le Pierre;
S'aporterai me fourke fiere.   256

BAUDONS:
Et je men gros baston d'espine,
Qui est chiés Bourguet, me cousine.

ROBINS:
Hé! Peronnele! Peronnele!

PERONNELE:
Robin, ies tu che? Quel nouvele?   260

ROBINS:
Tu ne sés? Marote te mande;
Et s'averons feste trop grande!

BAUDON:
Most certainly, by this head of mine!

ROBIN:
You will have a good time,   244
Fair gentlemen, if you come,
For Huart will be there as well as you,
And Peronnelle. That's a good crowd, isn't it?
And you will have wheat bread,   248
Good cheese and pure water.

BAUDON:
Well, dear cousin, lead us there!

ROBIN:
But you two should go that way,
And I'll go get Huart   252
And Peronnelle.

BAUDON:
                    Go then, go!

GAUTIER:
And we'll go that way
By the path towards the Pierre;[28]
And I'll bring my pitchfork.   256

BAUDON:
And I, my big hawthorn cudgel,
That's at my cousin Bourguet's house.

ROBIN:
Hey! Peronnelle! Peronnelle!

PERONNELLE:
Robin, is that you? What news?   260

ROBIN:
Don't you know? Marion asks for you;
We're going to have a lovely party!

PERONNELE:
Et qui i sera?

ROBINS:
                    Jou et tu;
Et s'arons Gautier le Testu,   264
Baudon et Huart et Marote.

PERONNELE:
Vestirai je me bele cote?

ROBINS:
Nennil, Perrote, nenil nient,
Car chis jupiaus trop bien t'avient.   268
Or te haste; je vois devant.

PERONNELE:
Va; je te sievrai maintenant,
Se j'avoie mes aigniaus tous.

LI CHEVALIERS:
Dites, bergiere, n'estes vous   272
Chele que je vi hui matin?

MARIONS:
Pour Dieu, sire, alés vo chemin;
Si ferés mout grant courtoisie.

LI CHEVALIERS:
Certes, bele, tres douche amie,   276
Je ne le di mie pour mal.
Mais je vois querant chi aval
.I. oisel a une sonnete.

MARIONS:
Alés selonc ceste haiete;   280
Je cuit que vous l'i trouverés.
Tout maintenant i est volés.

PERONNELLE:
    Who will be there?

ROBIN:
                            You and I;
    And we will have Gautier Bighead,   264
    Baudon and Huart and Marion.

PERONNELLE:
    Shall I put on my nice gown?

ROBIN:
    No, little Peronnelle, no need,
    For this jacket suits you very well.   268
    Do hurry; I will go on ahead.

PERONNELLE:
    Go on; I'd follow you right away,
    If I had all my lambs together.

THE KNIGHT:
    Tell me, shepherdess, aren't you   272
    The one I saw here this morning?

MARION:
    For God's sake, sir, go on your way;
    You will be acting most courteously.

THE KNIGHT:
    Indeed, fair one, sweet friend,   276
    I don't mean any harm.
    Actually I am looking down here
    For a bird with a bell.[29]

MARION:
    Go along this little hedge;   280
    I believe you will find it there.
    Just now it flew there.

LI CHEVALIERS:
Est, par amours?

MARIONS:
              Oïl, sans faille.

LI CHEVALIERS:
Certes, de l'oisel ne me caille,   284
S'une si bele amie avoie.

MARIONS:
Pour Dieu, sire, alés vostre voie,
Car je sui en trop grant frichon.

LI CHEVALIERS:
Pour qui?

MARIONS:
            Certes, pour Robechon.   288

LI CHEVALIERS:
Pour lui?

MARIONS:
          Voire, s'il le savoit,
Jamais nul jour ne m'ameroit,
Ne je tant rien n'aim comme lui.

LI CHEVALIERS:
Vous n'avés garde de nului   292
Se vous volés a mi entendre.

MARIONS:
Sire, vous nous ferés sousprendre.
Alés vous ent! Laissié me ester,
Car je n'ai a vous que parler.   296
Laissié me entendre a mes brebis.

LI CHEVALIERS:
Voirement sui je bien caitis

THE KNIGHT:
Is that so, I pray you?

MARION:
Yes, no doubt.

THE KNIGHT:
Indeed, I wouldn't care about the bird,   284
If I had such a pretty sweetheart.

MARION:
For God's sake, sir, go on your way,
For I quite shiver with fright.

THE KNIGHT:
For whom?

MARION:
Indeed, for my Robin.   288

THE KNIGHT:
For him?

MARION:
Indeed, if he knew of this,
Never again would he love me,
And I love no one as much as him.

THE KNIGHT:
You need not fear anyone   292
If you are willing to listen to me.

MARION:
Sir, you will get us caught.
Go away! Let me be,
For I have nothing to say to you.   296
Let me go tend to my sheep.

THE KNIGHT:
I am indeed a wretched fool

Quant je mec le mien sens au tien!

MARIONS:
Si en alés; si ferés bien.   300
Aussi oi je chi venir gent.
J'oi Robin flagoler au flagol d'argent,
Au flagol d'argent.
Pour Dieu, sire, or vous en alés!   304

LI CHEVALIERS:
Bergerete, a Dieu remanés;
Autre forche ne vous ferai.
Ha! Mauvais vilains, mar i fai!
Pour coi tues tu mon faucon?   308
Qui te donroit .i. horion
Ne l'aroit il bien emploiét?

ROBINS:
Ha, sire, vous feriés pechiét.
Peür ai que il ne m'escape.   312

LI CHEVALIERS:
Tien de loier ceste souspape,
Quant tu le manies si gent!

ROBINS:
Hareu! Diex! Hareu, bonne gent!

LI CHEVALIERS:
Fais tu noise? Tien che tatin!   316

MARIONS:
Sainte Marie! J'oi Robin!
Je croi que il soit entrepris.
Ains perderoie mes brebris
Que je ne li alasse aidier.   320
Lasse! Je voi le chevalier!
Je croi que pour moi l'ait batu.
Robin, dous amis, que fais tu?

To lower my wit to your level!

MARION:
    Then go away; you will be acting for the best.   300
    Besides, I hear people coming here.
    I hear Robin playing on his flageolet of silver,
    On his flageolet of silver.
    For God's sake, sir, do go away!   304

THE KNIGHT:
    Farewell then, little shepherdess;
    I will not force you any longer.[30]
    Hey! You wretched peasant, don't do that!
    Why are you killing my falcon?   308
    If someone gave you a smack
    Wouldn't it be well-applied?

ROBIN:
    Oh, sir, you would do wrong.
    I was afraid he might escape from me.   312

THE KNIGHT:
    Take this punch under the chin for payment,
    Since you handle him so gently!

ROBIN:
    Help! Oh, God! Help, good people!

THE KNIGHT:
    So you make a racket? Take this slap!   316

MARION:
    Holy Mary! I hear Robin!
    I believe he has been overcome.
    Rather I should lose my sheep
    Than not go to help him.   320
    Alas! I see the knight!
    I believe he has beaten him because of me.
    Robin, sweet friend, what's going on?

ROBINS:
Certes, douche amie, il m'a mort.   324

MARIONS:
Par Dieu, sire, vous avés tort
Qui ensi l'avés deskiré.

LI CHEVALIERS:
Et comment a il atiré
Mon faucon? Esgrardés, bregiere![31]   328

MARIONS:
Il n'en set mie la maniere.
Pour Dieu, sire, or li pardonnés!

LI CHEVALIERS:
Volentiers, s'aveuc moi venés.

MARIONS:[32]
Je non ferai.

LI CHEVALIERS:
               Si ferés voir.   332
N'autre amie ne voeil avoir,
Et voeil que chis chevaus vous porte.[33]

MARIONS:
Certes dont me ferés vous forche.
Robin, que ne me resqueus tu?   336

ROBINS:
Ha! Las! Or ai jou tout perdu!
A tart i venront mi cousin!
Je perc Marot, s'ai un tatin,
Et desquiré cote et sercot!   340

GAUTIERS:
Hé! Resveille toi Robin,
Car on en maine Marot, car on en maine Marot.

ROBIN:
    Sweetheart, he has certainly killed me.   324

MARION:
    In God's name, sir, you are wrong
    To have torn him up so.

THE KNIGHT:
    And how has he treated
    My falcon? Look, shepherdess!   328

MARION:
    He doesn't know the right way to do it:
    For heaven's sake, sir, pardon him!

THE KNIGHT:
    Gladly, if you will come with me.

MARION:
    I will not.

THE KNIGHT:
                Indeed you will.   332
    No other sweetheart do I want to have,
    And I want this horse to carry you off.

MARION:
    Indeed, then you will be doing me violence.
    Robin, why don't you rescue me?   336

ROBIN:
    Oh! Alas! Now I have lost everything!
    My cousins will come too late!
    I lose Marion, I've been slapped about,
    And I've torn both shirt and surcoat!   340

GAUTIER:
    Hey! Wake up, Robin,
    For someone is taking Marion away, for someone is
                            [taking Marion away.

ROBINS:
> Aimi! Gautier, estes vous la?
> J'ai tout perdu, Marote en va!   344

GAUTIERS:
> Et que ne l'alés vous reskeure?

ROBINS:
> Taisiés! Il nous couroit ja seure
> S'il en i avoit .iiii. chens.
> C'est uns chevaliers hors du sens,   348
> Qui a une si grant espee!
> Ore me donna tel colee
> Que je le sentirai grant tans.

BAUDONS:
> Se g'i fusse venus a tans,   352
> Il i eüst eü merlee!

ROBINS:
> Or esgardons leur destinee,
> Par amours, si nous embuissons
> Tout troi derriere ces buissons;   356
> Car je voeil Marion sekeure
> Se vous le m'aidiés a reskeure.
> Li cuers m'est .i. peu revenus.

MARIONS:
> Biau sire, traiés vous ensus   360
> De moi; si ferés grant savoir.

LI CHEVALIERS:
> Demisele, non ferai voir;
> Ains vous en menrai aveuc moi,
> Et si arés je sai bien coi.   364
> Ne soiiés envers moi si fiere!
> Prendés cest oisel de riviere
> Que j'ai pris. Si en mengeras.

ROBIN:
> Ai! Gautier, are you there?
> I have lost everything, Marion is gone!   344

GAUTIER:
> And why aren't you going to rescue her?

ROBIN:
> Be quiet! He would fall on us
> Even if there were four hundred of us.
> He's a knight gone wild,   348
> And he has such a huge sword!
> Just now he gave me such a blow
> That I will feel it for a long time.

BAUDON:
> If only I had come in time,   352
> There would have been a scuffle!

ROBIN:
> Now let us watch what happens to them,
> And, please, let us take cover,
> All three of us behind these bushes;   356
> For I want to help Marion,
> If you will assist me to rescue her.
> My courage has come back a little.

MARION:
> Fair sir, withdraw   360
> From me; it will be wiser.

THE KNIGHT:
> Young lady, I will do no such thing;
> Rather I will take you away with me,
> And I know what you shall have.   364
> Don't be so haughty towards me!
> Have some of this river fowl
> That I caught. Eat some of it.

MARIONS:
> J'ai plus chier mon froumage cras,   368
> Et men pain et mes bonnes poumes
> Que vostre oisel a tout les plumes;
> Ne de rien ne me poés plaire.

LI CHEVALIERS:
> Qu'est che? Ne porrai je dont faire   372
> Chose qui te viengne a talent?

MARIONS:
> Sire, sachiés certainement
> Que nenil; riens ne vous i vaut.

LI CHEVALIERS:
> Bergiere, et Diex vous consaut!   376
> Certes voirement sui je beste
> Quant a ceste beste m'areste!
> A Dieu, bergiere.

MARIONS:
>   A Dieu, biau sire.
> Lasse! Or est Robins en grant ire,   380
> Car bien me cuide avoir perdue.

ROBINS:
> Hou, hou!

MARIONS:
>   Dieus, c'est il qui la hue!
> Robin, dous amis, comment vait?

ROBINS:
> Marote, je sui de bon hait,   384
> Et garis puis que je te voi.

MARIONS:
> Vien donques cha, acole moi.

MARION:

    I prefer my rich cheese, 368
    And my bread and my good apples
    To your fowl with all its feathers;
    You cannot please me with anything.

THE KNIGHT:

    What is this? Will I be able to do nothing 372
    To please you then?

MARION:

    Sir, believe me that the answer
    Is no; nothing will be of any avail.

THE KNIGHT:

    Then, shepherdess, may God guide you! 376
    I must truly be a simpleton
    To have stopped to dally with this creature!
    Adieu, shepherdess.

MARION:

                Adieu, fair sir.
    Alas! Robin must be grief-stricken, 380
    For he certainly believes he has lost me.

ROBIN:

    Ho, ho!

MARION:

           Good God! It's he, calling for me!
    Robin, sweetheart, how are you?

ROBIN:

    Marion, I am of good cheer, 384
    And recovered, now that I see you.

MARION:

    Come here then and hug me.

ROBINS:
Volentiers, suer, puis qu'il t'est bel.

MARIONS:
Esgarde de cest sosterel   388
Qui me baise devant le gent!

BAUDONS:
Marot, nous sommes si parent;
Onques ne vous doutés de nous.

MARIONS:
Je ne le di mie pour vous,   392
Mais il par est si soteriaus
Qu'il en feroit devant tous chiaus
De no vile autretant comme ore.

ROBINS:
Et qui s'en tenroit?

MARIONS:
                        Et encore![34]   396
Esgarde comme est reveleus!

ROBINS:
Diex! Con je seroie ja preus
Se li chevaliers revenoit!

MARIONS:
Voirement, Robin? Que che doit   400
Que tu ne sés par quel engien
Je m'escapai?

ROBINS:
                Je le soi bien![35]
Nous veïsmes tout ton couvin.
Demandés Baudon, men cousin,   404
Et Gautier, quant t'en vi partir
S'il orent en moi que tenir.
Trois fois leur escapai tous .ii.

ROBIN:
Gladly, darling, since it pleases you.

MARION:
Look at this silly little fool   388
Who kisses me in front of other people!

BAUDON:
Marion, we are his relatives;
No need to fear us.

MARION:
I don't say it at all because of you,   392
But he is such a silly little fool
That he would just as soon do it before everyone
In our village, as he did it just now.

ROBIN:
And who would hold back?

MARION:
                              Another time!   396
See how bold he is!

ROBIN:
Good God! How brave I would be
If the knight came back!

MARION:
Really, Robin? How can it be   400
That you don't know by what trick
I escaped?

ROBIN:
            I know very well!
We saw everything you did.
Ask Baudon, my cousin,   404
And Gautier, if when I saw you leave,
They could hardly hold me back.
Three times I escaped them both.

GAUTIERS:
> Robin, tu ies trop corageus.   408
> Mais quant li cose est bien alee,
> De legier doit estre ouvliee,
> Ne nus ne le doit point reprendre.

BAUDONS:
> Il nous couvient Huart atendre   412
> Et Peronnele qui venront.
> Ou, vés les chi!

GAUTIERS:
>   Voirement sont.
> Di, Huart, as tu te chievrete?

HUARS:
> Oïl.

MARIONS:
>   Bien viegnes tu, Perrete!   416

PERONNELE:
> Marote, Dieus te beneïe!

MARIONS:
> Tu as esté trop souhaidie.
> Or est il bien tans de canter:

LI COMPAIGNIE:
> *Aveuc tele compaignie*   420
> *Doit on bien joie mener.*

BAUDONS:
> Somme nous ore tout venu?

HUARS:
> Oïl.

MARIONS:
>   Or pourpensons un jeu.

GAUTIER:

    Robin, you are very brave.   408
    But when the affair has gone well,
    It should be easily forgotten,
    No one need bother about it afterwards.

BAUDON:

    We should wait for Huart   412
    And Peronnelle, who are coming.
    Oh, here they are!

GAUTIER:

                Indeed they are.
    Say, Huart, do you have your bagpipe?

HUART:

    Yes.

MARION:

      How good that you came, Peronnelle!   416

PERONNELLE:

    God bless you, Marion!

MARION:

    You have been much wished for.
    Now is the time to sing:

THE COMPANY:

    With such company   420
    One must greatly rejoice.

BAUDON:

    Are we all here now?

HUART:

    Yes.

MARION:

    Now let us think of a game.

HUARS:
Veus tu as Roys et as Roïnes?   424

MARIONS:
Mais des jeus c'on fait as estrines,
Entour le veille du Noël.

HUARS:
A saint Coisne?

BAUDONS:
              Je ne voeil el.

MARIONS:
C'est vilains jeus; on i cunkie.   428

HUARS:
Marote, si ne riés mie.

MARIONS:
Et qui le nous devisera?

HUARS:
Jou, trop bien. Quiconques rira
Quant il ira au saint offrir,   432
Ens ou lieu saint Coisne doit sir.
Et qui en puist avoir, s'en ait.

GAUTIERS:
Qui le sera?

ROBINS:
      Jou.

BAUDONS:
            C'est bien fait.   436
Gautiers, offrés premierement.

GAUTIERS:
Tenés, saint Coisne, che present,

HUART:
Do you want to play Kings and Queens?   424

MARION:
Perhaps the games that one plays at holiday time,
On Christmas Eve.

HUART:
Saint Cosme's game?

BAUDON:
                    I want nothing else.

MARION:
That's a nasty game; one gets made fun of.   428

HUART:
Then don't laugh, Marion.

MARION:
But who will explain it to us?

HUART:
I will, and quite well. Whoever laughs
When he goes up to make an offering to the saint,   432
Must sit in turn in Saint Cosme's place.
And may the best one win.[36]

GAUTIER:
Who will be "it"?

ROBIN:
                    I will.

BAUDON:
                    Well done.   436
Gautier, make the first offering.

GAUTIER:
Saint Cosme, take this gift,

Et se vous en avés petit,
Tenés.

ROBINS:
　　Ou, il le doit! Il rit!

GAUTIERS:
　　Certes c'est drois.

HUARS:
　　　　　　　Marote, or sus.   440

MAROTE:
　　Qui le doit?

HUARS:
　　　　　　Gautiers li Testus.

MARIONS:
　　Tenés, saint Coisnes, biaus dous sire.

HUARS:
　　Diex, com ele se tient de rire!
　　Qui va apres? Perrote, alés!   444

PERONNELE:
　　Biau sire, sains Coisnes, tenés;
　　Je vous aporte che present.

ROBINS:
　　Tu te passes et bel et gent.
　　Or sus, Huart, et vous, Baudon.   448

BAUDONS:
　　Tenés, saint Coisne, che biau don.

GAUTIERS:
　　Tu ris, ribaus, dont tu le dois!

And, if you find it insufficient,
Here's some more.

ROBIN:
Hey, he loses! He's laughing!

GAUTIER:
All right, that's fair.

HUART:

Marion, your turn. 440

MARION:
Who lost?

HUART:

Gautier Bighead.

MARION:
Here, Saint Cosme, gentle good sir.

HUART:
Heavens, how she holds back from laughing!
Who's going next? Peronnelle, let's go! 444

PERONNELLE:
Fair sir, Saint Cosme, here;
I bring you this offering.

ROBIN:
You do that nicely.
Come on, Huart, and you, Baudon. 448

BAUDON:
Saint Cosme, take this fine gift.

GAUTIER:
You're laughing, you clown, so you lose!

BAUDONS:
  Non fach!

[GAUTIERS]:
          Huart apres!³⁷

HUARS:
                    Je vois.
  Ves chi deus mars.

GAUTIERS:³⁸
              Vous le devés.   452

HUARS:
  Or tout coi, point ne vous levés,
  Car encore n'ai je point ris.

GAUTIERS:
  Que ch'est, Huart? Est chou estris?
  Tu veus toudis estre batus.   456
  Mau soiiés vous ore venus!
  Or le paie tost sans dangier.

HUARS:
  Je le voil volentiers paier.

ROBINS:
  Tenés, sains Coismes, est che pais?   460

MARIONS:
  Ho! Singneur, chis jeus est trop lais;
  En est, Perrete?

PERONNELE:
                Il ne vaut nient.
  Et sachiés que bien apartient
  Que fachons autres festeletes.   464
  Nous sommes chi .ii. baisseletes
  Et vous estes entre vous .iiii.

BAUDON:
  Not so!

GAUTIER:
          Huart next!

HUART:
                    I'm coming.
  Here are two marcs.

GAUTIER:
                    You lose.   452

HUART:
  Now, hold on, don't get up,
  Because I didn't laugh yet.

GAUTIER:
  What is this, Huart? Is this a quarrel?
  You always want to be beaten up.   456
  You'll be sorry you came here!
  Now pay up and stop stalling.

HUART:
  I'll pay for it, willingly.[39]

ROBIN:
  Come on, Saint Cosme, shall we make peace?   460

MARION:
  Ho! Gentlemen, this game is too ugly;
  Isn't it, Peronnelle?

PERONNELLE:
                    It's not worth it.
  I think that we really should
  Find some other games.   464
  Here we are two girls
  And you are four among you.

GAUTIERS:
    Faisons .i. pet pour nous esbatre;
    Je n'i voi si bon.

ROBINS:
                           Fi, Gautier![40]   468
    Savés si bel esbanoiier
    Que devant Marote m'amie
    Avés dit si grant vilenie?
    Dehait ait par mi le musel   472
    A cui il plaist ne il est bel!
    Or ne vous aviegne jamais!

GAUTIERS:
    Je le lairai pour avoir pais.

BAUDONS:
    Or faisons .i. jeu.

HUARS:
                           Quel vieus tu?   476

BAUDONS:
    Je voeil, o Gautier le Testu,
    Jouer as Rois et as Roïnes;
    Et je ferai demandes fines
    Se vous me volés faire roy.   480

HUARS:
    Nenil, sire, par saint Eloi;
    Ains ira au nombre des mains.

GAUTIERS:
    Certes, tu dis bien, biaus compains,
    Et chieus qui chiet en .x. soit rois.   484

HUARS:
    C'est bien, de nous tous li otrois.
    Or cha! Metons nos mains ensanle.

GAUTIER:
>Let's fart to amuse ourselves.
>I don't see anything better to do.

ROBIN:
>Shame on you, Gautier! 468
>How can you joke like that
>And in front of Marion, my sweetheart,
>Say such an awful thing?
>Cursèd be the ugly mug 472
>Who finds it right and pleasing!
>You had better not ever do it again!

GAUTIER:
>I'll let it drop in order to have peace.

BAUDON:
>Now let's play a game.

HUART:
>Which one do you want? 476

BAUDON:
>I want, like Gautier Bighead,
>To play Kings and Queens;[41]
>And I will ask excellent questions
>If you all agree to make me the king. 480

HUART:
>No, sir, by Saint Eloi;
>It will be done by a countdown.

GAUTIER:
>Indeed, you're right, fair friend,
>And may whoever gets ten be king. 484

HUART:
>All right, we all agree.
>Come on! Let's put our hands together.

BAUDONS:
Sont eles bien? Que vous en sanle?
Li quiex commenchera?

HUARS:
Gautiers.   488

GAUTIER:[42]
Je commencherai volentiers.
Empreu.

HUARS:
Et deus.

ROBINS:
Et trois.

BAUDONS:
Et quatre.

HUARS:
Conte[43] apres, Marot, sans debatre.

MARIONS:
Trop volentiers: et .v.

PERONNELE:
Et .vi.   492

GAUTIERS:
Et .vii.

HUARS:
Et .viii.

ROBINS:
Et .ix.

BAUDONS:
Et .x.

BAUDON:
Are they right? What do you think?
Which of us will start?

HUART:
                              Gautier.   488

GAUTIER:
I'll start willingly.
One.

HUART:
     And two.

ROBIN:
          And three.

BAUDON:
               And four.

HUART:
Count next, Marion, without debate.

MARION:
Quite willingly: and five.

PERONNELLE:
                    And six.   492

GAUTIER:
And seven.

HUART:
          And eight.

ROBIN:
               And nine.

BAUDON:
                    And ten.

Enhenc, biau seigneur, je sui rois!

GAUTIERS:
Par le mere Dieu, chou est drois,
Et nous tout, je cuit, le volons.   496

ROBINS:
Levons le haut et couronnons!
Ho, bien est!

HUARS:
                    Hé, Perrete, or donne,
Par amours, en lieu de couronne
Au roi ton capel de festus.   500

PERONNELE:
Tenés, roi.

LI ROIS:
                    Gautiers li Testus,
Venés a court tantost, venés!

GAUTIERS:
Volentiers, sire. Commandés
Tel cose que je puisse faire,   504
Et qui ne soit a moi contraire.
Je le ferai tantost pour vous.

LI ROIS:
Di moi, fu tu onques jalous?
Et puis s'apelerai Robin.   508

GAUTIERS:
Oïl, sire, pour .i. mastin
Que j'oïs hurter l'autre fie
A l'uis de le cambre m'amie;
Si en soupechonnai .i. home.   512

LI ROIS:
Or sus, Robin!

So there, my lords, I am king, after all!

GAUTIER:
By the mother of God, that's fair,
And all of us, I believe, accept it.   496

ROBIN:
Let's raise him high and crown him!
There, that's good!

HUART:
                              Say, Peronnelle,
Please give your straw hat
To the king to use as a crown.   500

PERONNELLE:
Take it, your Majesty.

THE KING:
                              Gautier Bighead,
Come to the court, come right away!

GAUTIER:
Willingly, sire. Command me to do
Something that I can do,   504
And that would not be against my will.
I will do it right away for you.

THE KING:
Tell me, have you ever been jealous?
And then I will call Robin.   508

GAUTIER:
Yes, sire, because of a dog
That I heard the other day, knocking against
The door of my sweetheart's chamber;
For I suspected a man was there.   512

THE KING:
You're next, Robin!

ROBINS:

                    Rois, walecomme.
Demande moi che qu'il te plaist.

LI ROIS:

Robin, quant une beste naist,
A coi sés tu qu'ele est femele?   516

ROBINS:

Ceste demande est bonne et bele!

LI ROIS:

Dont i respon!

ROBINS:

                    Non ferai voir!
Mais se vous le volés savoir,
Sire rois, au cul li wardés.   520
El de mi vous n'en porterés.
Me cuidiés vous chi faire honte?

MARIONS:

Il a droit, voir.[44]

LI ROIS:

                    A vous k'en monte?

MARIONS:

Si fait car li demande est laide.   524

LI ROIS:

Marot, et je voeil qu'il souhaide
Son voloir.

ROBINS:

                Je n'os, sire.

LI ROIS:

                        Non?
Va, s'acole dont Marion,

ROBIN:
>   Welcome, Your Majesty.
> Ask me whatever pleases you.

THE KING:
> Robin, when a creature is born,
> How do you know if it's a female?   516

ROBIN:
> That's a nice question to ask!

THE KING:
> Then answer it!

ROBIN:
>   I most certainly will not!
> But if you want to know the answer,
> Lord King, look at its backside.   520
> You'll get nothing more from me.
> Did you think to embarrass me this way?

MARION:
> Really, he's right.

THE KING:
>   What do you care?

MARION:
> I care because the question is ugly.   524

THE KING:
> Marion, I want him to wish for
> His heart's desire.

ROBIN:
>   I don't dare.

THE KING:
>   No?
> Go on, hug Marion then,

Si douchement que il li plaise.   528

MARIONS:
Awar dou sot, s'il ne me baise!

ROBINS:
Certes, non fac.

MARIONS:
                              Vous en mentés.
Encore i pert il; esgardés!
Je cuit que mors m'a ou visage!   532

ROBINS:
Je cuidai tenir .i. froumage,
Si te senti je tenre et mole.
Vien avant, seur, et si m'acole
Par pais faisant.

MARIONS:
                              Va, dyable sos!   536
Tu poises autant comme .i. blos!

ROBINS:
Or, de par Dieu!

MARIONS:
                              Vous vous courchiés?
Venés cha, si vous rapaisiés,
Biau sire, et je ne dirai plus.   540
N'en soiés honteus ne confus.

LI ROIS:
Venés a court, Huart, venés.

HUARS:
Je voiss puis que vous le volés.

LI ROIS:
Or di, Huart, si t'aït Diex,   544

As tenderly as it pleases her.   528

MARION:
Look at that silly fool, if he doesn't kiss me.

ROBIN:
Indeed, not so.

MARION:
                    You're lying.
The mark is still there; look!
I think he's bitten me on the face!   532

ROBIN:
I thought I was holding a cheese,
And I smelled you soft and ripe.
Come, darling, and hug me
To make up.

MARION:
                    Go on, you foolish devil!   536
You're as heavy as a block!

ROBIN:
Now, for the love of God!

MARION:
                         Are you angry?
Come here, and calm yourself down,
Fair sir, and I won't say anything more.   540
Don't be ashamed or embarrassed.

THE KING:
Come to the court, Huart, come.

HUART:
I go, since you wish it.

THE KING:
Now tell us, Huart, so help you God,   544

Quel viande tu aimes miex.
Je sai bien se voir me diras.

HUARS:
Bon fons de porc pesant et cras
A le fort aillie de nois.   548
Certes, j'en mengai l'autre fois
Tant que j'en euch le menison.

BAUDONS:
Hé, Diex, con faite venison!
Huars n'en diroit autre cose.   552

HUARS:
Perrete, alés a court!

PERRETE:
                              Je n'ose.

BAUDONS:
Si feras, si Perrete. Or di,
Par cele fois que tu dois mi,
Le plus grant joie c'ainc eüsses   556
D'amours, en quel lieu que tu fusses.
Or di, et je t'escouterai.

PERRETE:
Sire, volentiers le dirai.
Par foi chou est quant mes amis,   560
Qui en moi cuer et cors a mis,
Tient a moi as cans compaignie,
Lés mes brebis, sans vilenie,
Pluseurs fois menu et souvent.   564

BAUDONS:
Sans plus?

PERRETE:
              Voire, voir!

Which food you like the best.
I'll know whether you're telling the truth.

HUART:
A good hind of pork, heavy and fat,
With a strong garlic walnut sauce.   548
Truly, I ate so much of it the other day
That I had the runs from it.

BAUDON:
Oh, my God, what a dainty dish!
Huart couldn't say anything more seemly.   552

HUART:
Peronnelle, go to the court!

PERONNELLE:
              I don't dare.

BAUDON:
Yes you do, Peronnelle. Now tell us,
Truly and faithfully,
About the greatest joy that you ever had   556
From love, wherever you might have been.
Now tell us, and I will listen to you.

PERONNELLE:
Sire, willingly I'll tell it:
Truly, it is when my friend,   560
Who has given me heart and self,
Keeps me company in the fields,
Next to my sheep, without offense,
Many and many a time.   564

BAUDON:
That's all?

PERONNELLE:
         Yes, truly.

HUARS:

                    Ele ment.

BAUDONS:
    Par le saint Dieu, je t'en croi bien.
    Marote, or sus, vien a court, vien.

MAROTE:
    Faites moi dont demande bele.   568

BAUDONS:
    Volentiers. Di moi, Marotele,
    Combien tu aimes Robinet,
    Men cousin, che joli varlet.
    Honnie soit qui mentira!   572

MARIONS:
    Par foi, je n'en mentirai ja.
    Je l'aim, sire, d'amour si vraie
    Que je n'aim tant brebis que j'aie,
    Nis cheli qui a aignelé.   576

BAUDONS:
    Par le saint Dieu, c'est bien amé!
    Je voeil qu'il soit de tous seü.

GAUTIERS:
    Marote, il t'est trop meskeü!
    Li leus emporte une brebis!   580

MAROTE:
    Robin, ceur i tost, dous amis,
    Anchois que li leus le mengüe!

ROBINS:[45]
    Gautier, prestés moi vo machue;
    Si verrés ja bacheler preu.   584
    Hareu! Le leu, le leu, le leu!
    Sui je li plus caitis qui vive?
    Tien, Marote.

HUART:

> She's lying.

BAUDON:

> By holy God, I believe you well.
> Marion, you're next, come to the court, come.

MARION:

> Ask me a nice question then. 568

BAUDON:

> Of course. Tell me, little Marion,
> How much you love little Robin,
> My cousin, this handsome lad.
> Shame on the one who lies! 572

MARION:

> In faith, I will never lie about that.
> I love him, sire, with a love so true
> That I love none of my sheep as much,
> Not even the one that just had a lamb. 576

BAUDON:

> By holy God, that is well loved!
> I want everyone to know it.

GAUTIER:

> Marion, something terrible has befallen you!
> The wolf is carrying away a sheep! 580

MARION:

> Robin, my dear, run there quickly
> Before the wolf eats her!

ROBIN:

> Gautier, lend me your club;
> And you will see a brave young man. 584
> Hareu! Wolf, wolf, wolf!
> Am I the most miserable man alive?[46]
> Here, Marion.

MAROTE:
>   Lasse, caitive!
> Commme ele revient dolereuse!   588

ROBINS:
> Mais esgar comme ele est croteuse!

MARIONS:
> Et comment tiens tu chele beste?
> Ele a le cul devers le teste.

ROBINS:
> Ne puet caloir; che fu de haste   592
> Quant je le pris. Marote, or taste
> Par ou li leus l'avoit aierse.

GAUTIERS:
> Mais esgar comme ele est chi perse.

MARIONS:
> Gautier, que vous estes vilains!   596

ROBINS:
> Marote, tenés le en vos mains,
> Mais wardés bien que ne vous morde.

MAROTE:
> Non ferai, car ele est trop orde;
> Mais laissié le aler pasturer.   600

BAUDONS:
> Sés tu de quoi je voeil parler,
> Robin? Se tu aimes autant
> Marotain, com tu fais sanlant,
> Certes je le te loëroie   604
> A prendre, se Gautiers l'otroie.

GAUTIERS:
> Jou l'otri.

MARION:
>   Poor, wretched thing!
> How she has come back all hurt!   588

ROBIN:
> But see how dirty she is!

MARION:
> And how you are holding the creature?
> She's all topsy-turvy!

ROBIN:
> It doesn't matter; I was in a hurry   592
> When I grabbed her. Marion, check her
> Where the wolf seized her.

GAUTIER:
> Look how blue she is here.[47]

MARION:
> Gautier, how vulgar you are!   596

ROBIN:
> Marion, take her in your arms,
> But don't let her bite you.

MARION:
> I won't take her, she's too dirty;
> Just let her go graze.   600

BAUDON:
> Do you know what I want to talk about,
> Robin? If you love Marion
> As much as you make believe,
> I would certainly advise you   604
> To make her yours, if Gautier agrees to it.

GAUTIER:
> It's agreeable to me.

ROBINS:
>   Et jou le voeil bien.

BAUDONS:
>   Pren le dont.

ROBINS:
>   Cha, est che tout mien?

BAUDONS:
>   Oïl, nus ne t'en fera tort.   608

MAROTE:
>   Hé, Robin! Que tu m'estrains fort!
>   Ne sés tu faire belement?

BAUDONS:
>   C'est grans merveille qu'il ne prent
>   De ches deus gens Perrete envie.   612

PERRETE:
>   Cui? Moi? Je n'en sai nul en vie
>   Qui jamais eüst de moi cure.

BAUDONS:
>   Si aroit, si, par aventure,
>   Se tu l'osoies assaier.   616

PERRETE:
>   Ba! Cui?

BAUDONS:
>   A moi ou a Gautier.

HUARS:
>   Mais a moi, tres douche Perrote.

GAUTIERS:
>   Voire, sire, pour vo musete?
>   Tu n'as ou monde plus vaillant.   620

ROBIN:
> And I wish it very much.

BAUDON:
Take her then.

ROBIN:
> So, is she all mine?

BAUDON:
Yes, no one will do you wrong.   608

MARION:
Hey! Robin, how tight you're holding me!
Can't you do it nicely?

BAUDON:
It's a marvel that seeing these two lovebirds
Doesn't make Peronnelle envious.   612

PERONNELLE:
Who? Me? I don't know of anyone alive
Who ever cared for me.

BAUDON:
There certainly would be one
If perhaps you dared try him.   616

PERONNELLE:
Bah! Who?

BAUDON:
> Either Gautier or me.

HUART:
Rather me, most sweet Peronnelle.

GAUTIER:
Indeed, sir, for your musette?
You have nothing in the world more valuable.   620

Mais j'ai au mains ronchi traiant,
Bon harnas et herche et carue,
Et si sui sires de no rue.
S'ai houche et sercot, tout d'un drap,   624
Et s'a me mere .i. bon hanap
Qui m'escherra s'elle moroit,
Et une rente c'on li doit
De grain seur .i. molin a vent,   628
Et une vake qui nous rent
Le jour assés lait et froumage.
N'a il en moi bon mariage?
Dites, Perrete?

PERRETE:

                  Oïl, Gautier,   632
Mais je n'oseroie acointier
Nului pour mon frere Guiot;
Car vous et li estes doi sot,
S'en porroit tost venir bataille.   636

GAUTIERS:

Se tu ne me veus, ne m'en caille.
Entendons a ces autres noches.

HUARS:

Di moi, c'as tu chi en ches boches?

PERONNELE:

Il i a pain, sel et cresson.   640
Et tu, as tu rien, Marion?

MARIONS:

Naie, voir, demande Robin —
Fors du froumage d'ui matin,
Et du pain qui nous demoura,   644
Et des poumes qu'il m'aporta.
Vés en chi se vous en volés.

GAUTIERS:

Et qui veut deus gambons salés?

But I have in my possession a draught-horse,
A good harness, harrow and plow,
And I am master of our street.
I have a tunic and a surcoat from the same cloth,   624
And my mother has a valuable goblet
That will fall to me when she dies,
And an income from a windmill
That is paid to her in grain,   628
And a cow that provides us everyday with
Much milk and cheese.
Am I not a good match?
What do you say, Peronnelle?

PERONNELLE:

                          Yes, Gautier,   632
But I wouldn't dare start up with
Anyone because of my brother Guiot;
For you and he are two fools,
And a fight could soon come out of it.   636

GAUTIER:
If you don't want me, I don't care.
Let's see about this other wedding.

HUART:
Tell me, what do you have in those bulges?[48]

PERONNELLE:
Some bread, salt and watercress.   640
And you, have you anything, Marion?

MARION:
Nothing really; ask Robin ——
Except for some cheese from this morning,
And some bread that's left,   644
And some apples that he brought me.
Here they are, if you want some.

GAUTIER:
And who wants two salted hams?

HUARS:
Ou sont il?

GAUTIERS:
Vés les chi tous pres.   648

PERONNELE:
Et jou ai deus froumages fres.

HUARS:
Di, de quoi sont il?

PERONNELE:
De brebis.

ROBINS:
Segneur, et j'ai des pois rotis.

HUARS:
Quides tu par tant estre quites?   652

ROBINS:
Naie, encor ai jou poumes quites.
Marion, en veus tu avoir?

MARIONS:
Nient plus?

[ROBINS]:
Si ai.

MARIONS:
Di me dont voir
Que chou est que tu m'as wardé.   656

ROBINS:
J'ai encore .i. tel pasté,
Qui n'est mie de lasté,
Que nous mengerons, Marote,
Bec a bec et moi et vous;   660

HUART:
Where are they?

GAUTIER:

They're right here. 648

PERONNELLE:
And I have two fresh cheeses.

HUART:
Say, what are they made from?

PERONNELLE:

From sheep's milk.

ROBIN:
My lords, I have some roasted peas.

HUART:
Do you think yourself quits for just that? 652

ROBIN:
Nay, I have some baked apples, too.
Marion, do you want to have some?

MARION:
You've nothing more?

ROBIN:

Yes, I do.

MARION:

Tell me then truly
What else you have saved for me. 656

ROBIN:
I still have one of those pies
With nothing poor about it,
That we shall eat, my Marion,
Mouth to mouth, both me and you; 660

Chi me ratendés, Marote,
Chi venrai parler a vous.
Marote, veus tu plus de mi?

MARIONS:
Oïl, en non Dieu.

ROBINS:
                          Et jou te di——   664
Que jou ai un tel capon
Qui a gros et cras crepon,
Que nous mengerons, Marote,
Bec a bec et moi et vous;   668
Chi me ratendés, Marote,
Chi venrai parler a vous.

MAROTE:
Robin, revien dont tost a nous.

ROBIN:
Ma douche amie, volentiers.   672
Et vous, mengiés endementiers
Que g'irai; si ferés que sage.

MARIONS:
Robin, nous feriemmes outrage.
Saches que je te voeil atendre.   676

ROBINS:
Non feras, mais fai chi estendre
Ten jupel en lieu de touaille,
Et si metés sus vo vitaille,
Car je revenrai maintenant.[49]   680

MARIONS:
Met ten jupel, Perrete, avant;
Aussi est il plus blans du mien.

PERONNELE:
Certes, Marot, je le voeil bien,

Wait for me here, my Marion,
Here I will come to talk to you.
Marion, do you want more from me?

MARION:
Yes, in God's name.

ROBIN:
                      Then I tell you —   664
That I have one of those capons
With a nice fat rump
That we shall eat, my Marion,
Mouth to mouth, both me and you;   668
Wait for me here, my Marion,
Here I will come to talk to you.

MARION:
Robin, come back to us quickly.

ROBIN:
Gladly, my sweet love;   672
And you others, eat in the meantime
While I'm gone; it makes better sense.

MARION:
Robin, it wouldn't be right.
Believe that I want to wait for you.   676

ROBIN:
Don't do that, but do spread out
Your cape here as a tablecloth,
And place all your victuals on it,
For I will be back shortly.   680

MARION:
Put your cape instead, Peronnelle;
It is much whiter than mine.

PERONNELLE:
Certainly, Marion, I am glad to,

Puis que vo volentés i est.   684
Tenés, veés le chi tout prest.
Estendé le ou vous le volés.

HUARS:
Or cha, biau segnieur, aportés,
S'il vous plaist, vo viande cha.   688

PERONNELE:
Esgar, Marote, je voi la,
Che me samble, Robin venant.

MARIONS:
C'est mon, et si vient tout balant.
Que te sanle? Est il bons caitis?   692

PERONNELE:
Certes, Marot, il est faitis,
Et de faire vo gré se paine.

MARIONS:
Awar les corneurs qu'il amaine!

HUARS:
Ou sont il?

GAUTIERS:
              Vois tu ches varlés   696
Qui la tienent ches .ii. cornés?

HUARS:
Par le saint Dieu, je les voi bien.

ROBINS:
Marote, je sui venus --— tien!
Or di, m'aimes tu de bon cuer?   700

MARIONS:
Oïl, voir.

Since it is your wish. 684
Take it, here it is all ready.
Spread it where you like.

HUART:
Now then, my lords, bring
Your food here, if you please. 688

PERONNELLE:
Look there, Marion, it seems to me
That I see Robin coming.

MARION:
You're right, and he's dancing as he comes.
What do you think? Isn't he a jolly fellow? 692

PERONNELLE:
Truly, Marion, he is good-looking,
And he does take pains to do your bidding.

MARION:
Look at the hornplayers he is bringing!

HUART:
Where are they?

GAUTIER:
Do you see those young men 696
Who are holding those two great horns?

HUART:
By holy God, I see them well.

ROBIN:
Marion, I have come — take this!
Now say, do you love me with all your heart? 700

MARION:
Yes, truly.

ROBINS:
                    Tres grant merchis, suer,
De che que tu ne t'en escuses.

MARIONS:
    Hé, que sont che la?

ROBINS:
                            Che sont muses
    Que je pris a chele vilete.   704
    Tien, esgar con bele cosete!

MARIONS:
    Robin, par amours, sié te cha,[50]
    Et chil compaignon seront la.

ROBINS:
    Volentiers, bele amie chiere.   708

MARIONS:
    Or faisons trestout bele chiere.
    Tien che morsel, biaus amis dous.
    Hé! Gautier, a quoi pensés vous?

GAUTIERS:
    Certes, je pensoie a Robin,   712
    Car se nous ne fuissons cousin,
    Je t'eüsse amee sans faille,
    Car tu es de trop bonne taille.
    Baudon, esgar quel cors chi a!   716

ROBINS:
    Gautier, ostés vo main de la!
    Et n'est che mie vo amie.

GAUTIERS:
    En es tu ja en jalousie?

ROBINS:
    Oïl, voir!

ROBIN:
>   Thank you very much, my darling,
> For not refusing to answer.

MARION:
> Hey, what are these?

ROBIN:
>   These are musettes
> That I got in that village.   704
> Here, see what a pretty little thing this is!

MARION:
> Robin, please, sit down here,
> And your companions over there.

ROBIN:
> Willingly, my dearest sweetheart.   708

MARION:
> Now let us make good cheer.
> Take this morsel, my darling.
> Hey! Gautier, what are you thinking about?[51]

GAUTIER:
> Indeed, I was thinking about Robin,   712
> Because if we weren't cousins,
> I would have loved you without a doubt,
> For you really are good-looking.
> Baudon, look what a figure she has here!   716

ROBIN:
> Gautier, take your hand away from there!
> She is not your sweetheart.

GAUTIER:
> Are you already so jealous of her?

ROBIN:
> Indeed yes!

MARIONS:

                    Robin, ne te doute.   720

ROBINS:

    Encore voi je qu'il te boute!

MARIONS:

    Gautier, par amours, tenés cois;
    Je n'ai cure de vo gabois.
    Mais entendés a nostre feste.   724

GAUTIERS:

    Je sai trop bien canter de geste.
    Me volés vous oïr canter?

BAUDONS:

    Oïl.

GAUTIERS:

            Fai moi dont escouter.
    Audigier, dist Raimberge, bouse vous di.   728

ROBINS:

    Ho! Gautier, je n'en voeil plus — fi!
    Dites, serés vous tous jours teus?
    Vous estes uns ors menestreus.

GAUTIERS:

    En mal eure gabe chis sos   732
    Qui me va blamant mes biaus mos.
    N'est che mie bonne canchons?

ROBINS:

    Nennil, voir.

PERRETE:

                Par amours, faisons
    Le tresque et Robins le menra,   736
    S'il veut, et Huars musera,
    Et chil doi autre corneront.

MARION:
>   Robin, have no fear.   720

ROBIN:
I still see him touching you!

MARION:
Gautier, please, behave yourself;
I don't care for your jokes.
Come now, let's get on with our party.   724

GAUTIER:
I can sing an epic song very well.
Do you want to hear me sing?

BAUDON:
Yes.

GAUTIER:
>   Listen to me then.
Audigier, said Raimberge, shit on you, I say.[52]   728

ROBIN:
Ho! Gautier, no more of that —— shame on you!
So, you're still acting up?
You sing like a filthy good-for-nothing.

GAUTIER:
To his misfortune this fool mocks me,   732
And goes criticizing my pretty words.
Isn't it a good song?

ROBIN:
Certainly not.

PERONNELLE:
>   I pray you all, let's do
A farandole, and Robin will lead it,   736
If he agrees, and Huart will play the musette,
And those other two will play their horns.

MARIONS:

Or ostons tost ches coses dont.
Par amour, Robin, or le maine.   740

ROBINS:

Hé, Dieus! Que tu me fais de paine!

MARIONS:

Or fai, dous amis, je t'acole.

ROBINS:

Et tu verras passer d'escole
Pour chou que tu m'as acolé.   744
Mais nous arons anchois balé,
Entre nous deus, qui bien balons.

MARIONS:

Soit, puis qu'il te plaist; or alons,
Et si tien le main au costé.   748
[53]Dieu, Robin, con c'est bien balé!

ROBINS:

Est che bien balé, Marotele?

MARIONS:

Certes! Tous li cuers me sautele,
Que je te voi si bien baler.   752

ROBINS:

Or voeil jou le treske mener.

MARIONS:

Voire, pour Dieu, mes amis dous.

ROBINS:

Or sus, biau segneur, levés vous!
Si vous tenés, g'irai devant.   756
Marote, preste moi ton gant,
S'irai de plus grant volenté.

MARION:
    Now then, let's clear all these things away.
    Lead it, Robin, I pray you.   740

ROBIN:
    Good heavens! How you do impose on me!

MARION:
    Do it, sweetheart, and I will give you a hug.

ROBIN:
    And you will see me surpass in skill
    Because you have embraced me.   744
    But first we will dance,
    Just the two of us, for we dance so well.

MARION:
    Very well, if you like; come on then,
    But keep your hand so to the side.   748
    Heavens! Robin, that was well-danced!

ROBIN:
    Was that well-danced, my little Marion?

MARION:
    Certainly! My heart jumps like mad
    When I see you dance so well.   752

ROBIN:
    Now I wish to lead the farandole.

MARION:
    For Heaven's sake, of course, my darling.

ROBIN:
    Come, fair lords, stand up!
    Place yourselves and I will lead.   756
    Marion, lend me your glove,[54]
    And I will go with the greatest good will.[55]

PERONNELE:
  Dieu, Robin, que ch'est bien alé!
  Tu dois de tous avoir le los.   760

ROBINS:
  Venés apres moi, venés le sentele,
  Le sentele, le sentele, lés le bos.

PERONNELLE:
Heavens, Robin, how well it went!
You should be praised by all.   760

ROBIN:
Follow me, come down the path,
The path, the path along the wood.

NOTES

1. The word *testu* can be translated as "having a big head" or as "headstrong, stubborn." Adam is perhaps playing with the double meaning here. In the *Jeu du Pélerin*, not written by Adam, the author favors the first definition for Gautier's nickname and the uses the second meaning for a rhyme (see verses 51-52). Although Adam indicates no clear preference for one or the other meaning, such nicknames based on corporal abnormalities were common, as the necrology from Arras testifies (see introduction).

2. Manuscript reads *maine n'ent*.

3. An untranslatable refrain, similar to "tra la la" in English.

4. Sections in single quotes indicate that they are sung.

5. Henry emends this verse to read *Sire, j'en vi je ne sai kans*, thereby correcting the syllable count. However, since the correction is a conjecture and *Pa* contains the same reading as *P* (supporting the supposition that the two versions descend from the same copy), I have retained the hypometric reading. On the other hand, I have accepted Henry's argument for the addition of an *e* to correct the hypometric verse 29.

6.   Langlois amends to *herens* and Varty to *hairens* because
      of the play on words. Dufournet accepts the reading of
      P, surmising that the peasant pronunciation is enough
      to confuse the two words. See Dufournet ed. 136.

7.   Marion is either deliberately misunderstanding the
      knight, who of course is not speaking of songbirds but
      of game birds, in order to tease him, or is innocently
      unaware of why he has a falcon on his arm. More
      "misunderstandings" follow.

8.   The play here is on *ane*, meaning duck, and *asne* (the *s*
      is silent), meaning donkey.

9.   Another misunderstanding: the Knight says *hairon*
      (heron) and Marion understands *heren* ("herring"). A
      contemporary American southern accent could confuse
      these two English words today.

10.   Rubric is repeated needlessly in *P* before this verse.

11.   Metathesis of the *r* is very frequent in Picard. Note also
      fourment (for *froment*) in v. 248.

12.   A French bagpipe with the wind supplied with a
      bellows rather than a blowpipe.

13.   According to Langlois, the bodice of a loose-fitting
      dress served as a pocket (Langlois ed. 60).

14.   Manuscript reads *deure*.

15.   Scribe omits *s* in subject case proper name.

16.   The scribe here wrote Marion's cry in red with the
      rubric spelling *Robins* and wrote Robin's rubric in
      black with no *s*. I have restored the words to their
      proper places.

17.   An untranslatable refrain.

18. An untranslatable refrain.

19. Manuscript reads *amis dous*.

20. Dufournet provides an alternate translation "par le sein de Dieu," taking the exclamation as an example of the vulgarity of the peasants (Dufournet ed. 15-16).

21. Either Marion herself does not know the difference between an aristocratic leather hunting glove and a peasant's mitten, or between a hunting falcon and a kite, or she chooses these simpler concepts to explain the knight's visit to Robin who is not likely to be familiar with the aristocratic vocabulary.

22. *La choule* is a game similar to lacrosse, and, according to Guy, it was a rough, dangerous game. Thus Robin's fatigue and Marion's praise are warranted.

23. Robin performs a series of dance movements or acrobatics according to Marion's requests. Unfortunately, knowledge of the exact nature of these dances has been lost, although Françoise Ferrand hazards a guess (see bibliography).

24. Manuscript reads *au seraiu*. The preferred reading is from *Pa*.

25. The meaning of *seriaus* is unclear. Langlois claims not to have seen any other occurrence of this word and although he translates it as "assemblée du soir," he admits that he doubts the correctness of that translation. No other editor of this text has come up with a better suggestion.

26. Robin addresses his friends here as *signeur* (nominative plural). It appears to be an aristocratic affectation, and it recurs many times in the text. I have translated it variously as "gentlemen," "lords," or "my lords."

27. *Menestrel*, though originally the title for a poet-musician who served in a lord's household, came to be appropriated by ordinary, errant *jongleurs* who literally gave the word a bad name, and it became a pejorative term meaning "liar, false one, debauched one," etc. (Faral 103-18).

28. A place name.

29. A trained falcon would wear a bell so that he could be easily found again.

30. The knight withdraws and comes upon Robin who is holding his falcon maladroitly.

31. *Esgrardés* is unusual; *A* and *Pa* have *Esgardés*.

32. The rubrics for Marion's refusal and the knight's reply each follow the bit of dialogue instead of preceding it. For example (with original punctuation):
    Je non ferai MARIONS
    Si feres voir: LI CHEVALIERS.
    Nautre amie ne voeil avoir
    The scribe makes this error several times in the manuscript, and on two occasions even forgets the rubric. I have corrected the placement of the rubric to conform with the rest of the text.

33. One would expect the Picard form *porche* and some editors emend to this form, but it appears in none of the manuscripts, (both *Pa* and *A* have the pseudo-rhyme *porte / force*), and I have thus left the reading of *P* as is.

34. Again the rubric MARIONS follows the line of speech.

35. *Soi* is unusual. *Pa* has *sai*.

36. In this game, the offerings made were derisory or ridiculous, and the "saint" made distorted faces to get the person offering to laugh. If one laughed, one became "it," taking the place of the saint. See Hard af Segerstad's article for attestations of Saint Cosme's game.

37. The attribution of this speech to Gautier comes from *Pa*. In *P*, the verse reads as follows (including original punctuation):
    BAUDONS
    Non fach : Huart apres
    Je vois . HUARS .
    Thus, although *Huart apres* is attributed to Baudon, *Je vois* appears to be correctly attributed to Huart with the rubric following the speech, an error previously noted in relation to v. 332.

38. Manuscript *P* carries the rubric LI ROIS, an obvious error in anticipation of the game to follow the present one. I have substituted *Pa*'s attribution of this speech to Gautier. In *A* the entire verse is attributed to Huart.

39. Apparently Huart makes a threatening gesture, which makes Robin's next speech logical.

40. *Fi Gautier* is actually placed at the end of Gautier's speech, before Robin's rubric. I have joined it to the rest of Robin's speech as in *Pa* and *A*.

41. The proper name of the game, according to Langlois, is "Le Roi qui ne ment," an aristocratic truth game of the 13th and 14th centuries in which questions concerning love and one's lovers must be answered, and wit and repartee are valued. See Langlois's article in *Mélanges Chabaneau* for attestations of the game.

42. Scribe omits *s* in subject case proper name.

43. Manuscript reads *Eonte apres* — a confusion between capital *c* and *e*.

44. Manuscript reads *il a droit voir a vo*. The scribe probably began writing the king's line *a vous k'en monte* before writing the rubric, but failed to scratch out *a vo* after having caught his mistake.

45. The rubric in the manuscript is MAROTE; I have emended to ROBINS.

46. Antiphrastic sense. Note the variants in *Pa* and *A*: *li plus hardis* and *le plus hardi*.

47. Gautier is playing with the double meaning of *perse*: blue (or bruised), and pierced (pointing to her sexual organs). He thus merits Marion's reproach. See Varty, "Le Mariage" 291.

48. He points to Peronnelle's bodice where she stores food just as Marion does. Probable erotic word play as well.

49. Manuscript reads: *Car je revenrai certes lues* which rhymes with the first line of the first interpolation (see Appendix). I have adopted the reading from *Pa. A* ends the line: *tout errant*.

50. Manuscript reads: *Par amours et si te sié cha*. Like other editors, I have preferred the reading from *Pa* and *A*, for the verse as it reads in *P* introduces the second interpolation (see Appendix).

51. Gautier has obviously touched Marion inappropriately by putting his arm around her waist or something similar.

52. A line from a ribald mock epic poem. See Langlois ed. 68 and Dufournet ed. 151.

53. The rubric MARIONS is repeated before this line, perhaps to indicate the passage of time during the dance.

54. Although Marion substituted "mitten" for "glove" in verse 122, here Robin obviously knows the aristocratic term. Many see in this a continuation of the parody of aristocratic manners (like the use of the address "lords"), as ladies offered their gloves or sleeves to their favorite knights at tournaments as love-pledges.

55. Langlois explains how the dance is done: "Robin tient de la main droite le gant que Marion vient de lui donner; de sa main gauche il prend la main gauche de Marion, qui a sa main droite dans celle de Gautier. Après Gautier vient Perrette, puis Baudon. La farandole fait deux ou trois fois le tour de la scène, pendant que Huart et les corneurs jouent; puis elle disparait, ainsi que les musiciens" (Langlois ed. 68).

Melodies of Le Jeu de Robin et Marion

No.1 - Lines 1-8

m'ai - me,   Ro - bins   m'a,   Ro - bins   m'a

de - man - de - e   si m'a - ra.

No.2 - Lines 9-10

THE KNIGHT

Je   me   re - pai - roi - e   du   tour -

noi - e - ment,   Si   trou .- vai   Ma -

ro - te   seu - lete   au   cors gent.

No.3a - Lines 11-12

MARION

Hé!   Ro - bin,   se   tu   m'ai - mes,

Par   a - mours, mai - ne m'ent.

No.3b - Lines 18-19

THE KNIGHT

Hé! Ro - bin, se tu m'ai - mes,

Par a - mours, mai - ne m'ent.

No.4 - Lines 83-84

MARION

Vous per - dés vo pai - ne, sire Au - bert.

Je n'a - me - rai au - trui que Ro - bert.

No.5 - Lines 90-91

MARION

Ber - ge - ron - ne - te sui mais j'ai

A - mi bel et coin - te et gai.

No.6 - Lines 95-100

gie - re   tant   be - le

ne   vit   roys.   Hé!

Trai - ri   de-lu - riau   de-lu - riau   de-lu -

rie - le,   Trai - ri   de - lu -

riau   de-lu - riau   de-lu - rot.

No.7 - Lines 101-108

MARION

Hé! Ro - be - chon,   leu - re

leu - re va,   Car   vien   a   moi,

leu - re   leu - re   va,   S'i - rons   jeu -

er,   dou   leu - re   leu - re   va,   Dou

ROBIN

leu - re   leu - re   va.   Hé!   Ma - ri -

on,   leu - re   leu - re   va,   Je   vois   a

toi,   leu - re   leu - re   va,   S'i -

rons   jeu - er,   dou   leu - re   leu - re

va,   Dou   leu - re   leu - re   va.

No.8 - Lines 158-159

No.9 - Lines 170-180

moi, vos - tre cha - pe - let.

MARION

Vo - len - tiers, mendouc a - mi - et.

No.10 - Lines 185-208

MARION

Ro - bin, par l'a - me ten pe - re,

Sés tu bien a - ler du piet?

ROBIN

O - ïl, par l'a - me me me - re.

Res - gar - de, comme il me siet:

A - vant et ar - rie - re, Be - le,

O - ïl, par l'a - me me me - re,

Mais j'ai trop mains de cha - viaus,

De - vant que der - rie - re, Be - le,

de - vant que der - rie - re.

No.11 - Lines 302-303

J'oi Ro - bin fla- go - ler au fla -

gol d'ar - gent, Au fla - gol d'ar - gent.

No.12 - Lines 341-342

No.13 - Lines 420-421

No.14a - Lines 657-662

mi - e de las - té,   Que nous men - ge -
rons, Ma - ro - te, Bec a bec et moi et
vous;   Chi me ra - ten - dés, Ma - ro - te,
Chi ven - rai par - ler a vous.

No. 14b - Lines 665-670

ROBIN

Que jou ai un tel ca - pon   Qui a
gros et cras cre - pon,   Que nous men - ge -
rons, Ma - ro - te, Bec a bec et moi et

vous; Chi me ra - ten - dés, Ma - ro - te,

Chi ven - rai par - ler a vous.

No. 15 - Line 728

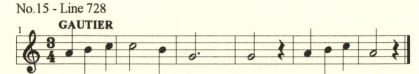

GAUTIER

Au - di - gier, dist Raim - ber - ge, bou - se vous di.

No. 16 - Lines 761-762

ROBIN

Ve - nés a - pres moi, ve - nés le sen-

te - le, Le sen - te - le, le sen - te - le, lés le bos.

No.X1 - Line 100

No.X2 - Line 108

VARIANTS

Spelling variations are generally restricted to the more interesting ones. The reading from the base manuscript *P* is separated from the variant by a bracket. Words that have been omitted are shown in parentheses, but the word *omitted* indicates a missing line. If the variants of a line of verse are identical in the two manuscripts, this is shown by the word *same* in the second column.

Pa		*A*	
Title Li jeus du bergier et de la bergiere		*The title* Mariage de Robin et de Marote *is not contemporary to the text, nor is the list of characters which follows*	
Speakers indicated by an initial; list of initials and speakers at bottom of f. 140		*First verse is preceded by the introduction* Marote chante	
R.Robins.M.Marions.G. Gautiers.P.Perrete. B.Baudons.H.Huars.li chevaliers			
		4	D'escarlate] De burel et
		5	*omitted*
		10	Marote] bergiere
		14	P.a.] Et p.a.
15	(douche), contés] ditez		
21	(bien)	21	J'a.] Car j'a.
		25	Di moi] Or me di
26	les] ces	26	*same*
		27	j'en ai veü ne s.] oïl je ne s. pas
		28	E. i a] E. en a
		29	C.] Et c.
30	*omitted*		
32	point] pas	32	*same*

	Pa		*A*
		35	C'est] Est-ce
36	J'en vi ier] Hier en vi		
40	Di moi v. tu n.] Di v. tu ci n.		
41	Hairons] Herens	41	Hairons] Harens
		42	n'en vi nes un] ne vi harens
		44	taiien c.] tante a c.
		44/5	*inserted between these two verses*: L'en en vent assez a Paris
45	esbaubis] abaubis	45	sui jou esbaubis] ne sai je que dire
		45/6	*inserted between these two verses*: Ne doi avoir talent de rire
46	N'ainc m. je ne f.] Car ainc m. ne f.	46	N'ainc m. je ne] Onques m. ne
51	ele] il		
54	de d.] grant d.	54	de d.] biau d.
		55	A] En
		61	Deseur] Ne de
63	Chi v. au vespre] Il v. au soir	63	*same*
64	et p.u.] ci p.u.	64	toudis et] tous les jors
65	Chi] Et	65	*same*
		68	Que il m'a. a p.] Qu'il m'a. ore a p.
		74	A p. que il] Par .i. p. qu'il
75	regiete] regetent	75	regiete] regibe
79	traiés] fuiés	79	S.t.] T. vous s.
81	vos] cis	81	*omitted*
		84	autrui] autre
87/8	*reversed*		
		91	b. et c.] c. et b.

	Pa		A
95/6	*r u b r i c* L I CHEVALIERS	95/6	*same*
		95	T.d.d.d.] T.d.d.
		96	T.d.d.d.] T.d.d.
97	jou] me	97	jou] grant
		98	tant] plus
		99	Hé t.d.d.d.] T.d.d.
		100	T.d.d. delurot] T.d. luroy
101	deure leure va] deluryva	101	deure l. va] leur l. va
102	l.l. va] l.l. y va		
103	d.l.l. va] d.l.l. y va	103	dou leure leure va] l. doleur va
104	d.l.l. va] d.l.l. y va	104	dou leure leure va] doleur va
105	leure leure va] deure leuriva	105	leure leure va] doleur va
106	leure leure va] leure leuriva	106	leure leure va] doleur va
107	d.l. leure va] d.l. leuriva	107	dou leure leure va] doleureure va
108	d.l. leure va] d.l. leuriva	108	dou leure leure va] dolereure va
		112	cote] houce
114	trop] moult		
		116	Et] Mes
119	m. a m.] m. en m.	119	ne le tien m.] ne le tiens m.
120	Par chi vint .i. h.] Yci fu uns h.	120	*same*
		124	a. mais p.] a. et p.
		125	(te)
126	M. tu] M. car tu		
127	a tans] au camps	127	(i)
		128	ne jou ne] ne moi ne
130	(mis)		
131	f. partis s.] f. alés s.		

	Pa		*A*
132	n. te c.] n. t'en c.		
135	V. si te sié encoste m.] Mais v. cha seoir delés m.	135	*same*
		141	Du froumage chi en mon sain] En mon sain .i. pou de fromage
		142	*omitted*
		143	des p.] les p.
144	D. que c.] D. com c.	144	*same*
		146	Quant t.] Se t.
148	o. eüst du] o. avoit du	148	q. ore eüst] q. eust ore
		149	Te taiien] Ta tante
151	*omitted*	151	as quieverons] a ses chevrons
154	p. lassee] p. enflee		
156	(Di), Robin] Robinet		
160	Di R.] R. di		
		161	Naie v.] Nennil v.
		163	Dusqu'a ja q.] Jusques tant q.
164	Ains le m.] Mais m. le		
		166	c. je] c. et je
167	jou e.] je t'e.	167	*same*
		171	(le)
		172	*omitted*
		174/5	*inserted between these two verses*: M'en iert il mieus se je l'i met *(repeated)*
175	(et)	175	*same*
179	*this verse is repeated*		
		180	V.m. douc a.] V. ci m.a.
		184	tu point oï]tu pas oï

Pa	A
	186 b. aler du p.] b. baler du p.
187 Oïl] Marote	
188 Resgarde comme il me siet] J'en venrai moult a chief	
194 v. mout b.] v. trop b.	
	198 C. nous f. le t. des b.] C. me f. le t. du b.
200 e. con tu] e. que tu	200 t. ensi c.] t. arasinc c.
	202/3 *inserted between these two verses:* MAROTE: Robin par l'ame ton pere/ Sés tu fere le touret ROBIN: Ouil par l'ame ma mere/ Ra il en moi biau vallet/ Devant et derriere/ Bele, devant et derriere
204 Sés tu] Veus tu	204 au s.] as s.
213 f. par a.] f. a a.	
214 g'irai] j. vois	214 *same*
215 au grant b.] au gros b.	215 *same*
	216/9 *attributed to Marion*
	216 Et si amenrai chi B.] Va et amaine o toi B.
	217 Se trouver le puis] Se tu le trueves
	227 Je ne] Saches je ne
	229 (tost), biau cousin] b. dous c.
	234 *pronounced by Gautier and Baudon to* battu
	235 *pronounced by*

	Pa		*A*
			Gautier and Baudon
		236	Signeur escoutés un p.] Por Dieu soufrez vous .i. p.
		240	me d.] m'en d.
242	*attributed to Baudon,* S'il revient] S'il y vient	242	*p r o n o u n c e d b y Gautier and Baudon*
243	*attributed to Gautier*		
		244	averés t.] a. ja t.
248	Et s'averés] Et s'averons		
		250	*attributed to Gautier*
251	(deus)		
253	Va don va *attributed to Gautier*		
		254/6	*attributed to Baudon*
254	i. par deça] i. d'autre part	254	Et nous en irons] Et je m'en irai
255	d. le Pierre] d. le pire	255	d. le Pierre] d. la ville
256	S'aporterai] Si porterai		
		257/8	*attributed to Gautier*
		257	m. gros b.] m. grant b.
		262	Et s'averons] Car nous aurons
		263	Et q. i s. J. et tu] Q. i s. Et j. et tu
		265	B. et H.] H. et B.
		267	n. nient] n. point
275	f. mout g.c.] f. trop g.c.	275	*same*
278	M. je vois querant c.a.] M. veïstez vous c.a.		
280	ceste h.] cele h.	280	*same*

	Pa		*A*
281	Je cuit q.v. l'i t.] Je croi q.v. le t.	281	*same*
		282	e. volés] e. alés
284	o. ne me] o. poi me	284	*same*
		286	(sire), alés v.] alez en v.
287	en t. grant f.] en t. mal f.		
		288	P. qui] P. quoi
291	Ne je t.r. n'a.] Ne je n'a.r.t.	291	Ne je t.r. n'a. c. lui] Ne je n'a. r.t.c. Robin
294	v. nous f.] v. me f.		
300	A. oi je] A. voi je	300	*same*
302/3	flagol] flajot	302/3	flagol] flagieu
		304	Pour Dieu s. or v.] Biau s. car v.
		305	B. a D.] B. et a D.
		308	mon f.] cel f.
		310	Ne l'a. il b. emploiét] Il a. moult b. esploitié
		312	P. ai q.] J'ai grant paor q.
314	(le)		
316	Fais tu noise] En grouces tu	316	n.t.] n. or t.
		318	s.e.] s. la e.
319	Ains perderoie] Anchois perdroie	319	*same*
		320	ne li alasse a.] ne l'alaisse a.
		322	m. l'ait b.] m. l'a b.
335	Certes d.] Par Dieu d.		
340	Et d.] S'ai d.		
		341/2	*attributed to Baudon*
343	Aimi] Amis	343	Aimi] Baudoul
345	*attributed to Baudon*, l'alés vous r.] l'alons	345	l'alés v. reskeure] l'alons nous secorre

Pa	A

nous r.

346	c. ja s.] c. tous s.		
349	Qui a u. si grant e.] Si a u. si longue e.	349	Qui a] Si a
		350	Or me d. tel c.] Il me d. si grant c.
351	grant t.] lonc t.		
352/3	*attributed to Gautier*	352/3	*same*
		357	sekeure] resqueurre
		358	Se vous le m'aidiés a reskeure] Si le m'aiderez a sequeurre
		365	Ne s. envers moi] Or ne me s. plus
		366	Prendés c.] Pren suer c.
		369	p. et m.] p. a m.
373	te viengne] te vient	373	te v.] vous v.
375	Q. nenil r.] Q. r. nule		
381	(me)		
		382	c'est il q.] est il ce q.
		382/3	*inserted between these two verses*: MAROT: Robin. ROBIN: Marot.
		383	(Robin), c.v.] c. te v.
		385	Et g.] Et tous g., (je)
388	Esgarde] Esgardés		
390/1	*attributed to Gautier*	390/1	*same*
		390	si p.] tuit p.
391	v. doutés de n.] v. caille de n.		
396	Et] Bé	396	Et] Ba
397	Esgarde] Esgardés	397	Esgarde] Esgardez
		398/407	*omitted*
398	D. con je] D. que j.		
400	q. che d.] ce q.d.		

Pa		*A*	
404	Demandés Baudon] Demande Gautier		
405	Gautier] Baudon		
406	S'il o.] Il n'o.		
408/11	*attributed to Baudon*	408/11	*attributed to Marion*
		408	trop c.] moult c.
		409	(quant)
411	n. ne le d. reprendre] n. ni d. apres entendre	411	*same*
412/4	*attributed to Marion to* chi	412/4	*attributed to Robin to* chi
		412	Il n.] Si n.
414	*second half of verse attributed to Baudon*	414	Ou vés l.c.] Oez l.c., *second half of verse attributed to Marion*
415	*attributed to Baudon*	415	*attributed to Robin*
		416	B. viegnes tu P.] B. veingnez vous P.
417	D. te b.] D. vous b.		
418/21	*attributed to Robin*		
		420/1	*attributed to Marion*
		420	Aveuc tele c.] En si bonne c.
		423/4	*attributed to Gautier*
423	*latter part of verse attributed to Baudon*	423	Oïl] Ouil voir
424	R. et] R. u	424	R. et] R. ou
425/6	*attributed to Baudon*	425/6	*no rubric*
425	M. des j.] M. as j.		
		427	*first part of verse no rubric, latter part attributed to Robin*
428	C.v.j.] C. uns v.j.		
		429	*attributed to Perrete*
430	*attributed to Baudon*		
		431/4	*attributed to Baudon*
433	(Ens)	433	(Ens), (doit), sir] seu

	Pa		*A*
435	*third rubric* H	435	*second rubric* BAUDOIL, *third rubric* GAUTIER
		436	*rubric* HUART
		437/9	*no rubric*
439	Ou] Ho	439	*latter part under rubric* PERRETE, Ou] Hé
		440	*first rubric* MAROTE, (Marote or sus)
		441	*entire verse attributed to Huart*
		443/4	*attributed to Robin*
443	t. de r.] t. bien de r.		
		449	*omitted*
		450	*attributed to Robin*
		451	*entire verse attributed to Baudon*
		452	*entire verse attributed to Huart*
455/8	*attributed to Baudon*	455/8	*attributed to Robin*
		455	Que ch'est H.] Qu'est ce H.
		456	v. toudis] v. tous jors
		456/7	*reversed*
		458	p. tost s. dangier] p. tout s. deignier
460	pais] plais	460	*same*
		464	Q. fachons] Q. faisons
		470	Que d.] Et d.
		472	Dehait a.] Maudehais a., (mi)
		473	ne il e.b.] n'a qui e.b.
476	*first rubric* P, *second rubric* M	476	*first rubric* MAROTE, *second rubric* ROBIN

Pa		A	
477/8	*attributed to Perette*	477/8	*attributed to Marion*
		479/80	*attributed to Gautier*
481/2	*attributed to Gautier*	481/2	*attributed to Robin*
481	N.s. par saint Eloi] N.s. foi que vous doi	481	*same*
483/4	*attributed to Huart*	483/4	*same*
485/6	*attributed to Gautier*	485/6	*attributed to Baudon*
		485	(tous)
487/8	*attributed to Huart*	487/8	*attributed to Robin*
488	*latter part under rubric* R		
490	*second rubric* P	490	*third rubric* BAUDOUL, *fourth rubric* ROBIN
491	Conte a. Marot] Contés a. tost	491	*attributed to Robin*
		492/3	*attributed to Marion*
493	*first rubric* H, *second rubric* G		
495/6	*attributed to Huart*	495/8	*attributed to Marion to middle of v. 498*
496	je cuit] je croi	496	tout je cuit] tous ce croi
497/8	*attributed to Gautier to middle of v. 498*		
		498	H. bien e.H.P. or d.] H. bon e.H.P. en quar me d.
		498/500	*attributed to Robin from mid. v. 498*
(*Pa consistently replaces rubric* LI ROIS *with* B *for Baudon who is playing the king*)			
501/2	*rubric* B *from middle of v. 501*	501/2	*rubric* BAUDOUL *from middle of v. 501*
505/6	*inserted between these two verses*: Mais que		

Pa		*A*	
	de ci ne me remu/ Ne ne bouch men doit u fu		
		506	f. tantost pour vous] f. se j'onques puis
		506/7	*inserted between these two verses*: Gautier premierement te ruis/ Que tu dies ci devant nous
507/8	*rubric* B	507/8	*rubric* LE ROI PARLE
		507	Di moi fu tu onques] S'onc fus de t'amie j.
513	*first rubric* B	513	*first rubric* LE ROI PARLE, (walecomme)
		514	demande m.] commande m.
515/6	*rubric* B		
515	u. beste] u. vake		
518	*first rubric* B		
521	El de mi vous n'en] Nel de moi n'en	521	El de mi vous n'en] Ja plus de moi n'en
		522	(vous)
523	*second rubric* B, v. k'en monte] v. c'amonte	523	v. k'en m.] v. que m.
525/6	*rubric* B		
526/8	*third rubric of v. 526 through v. 528* B		
		527	V. s'a. d. M.] V. d. s'a. M.
		528	Si d.q.] Bien d. si q.
529	Awar] Awa	529	Awar] Esgar
530	Certes non fac V. en m.] Non fais voir Et v. y m.	530	V. en m.] V. i m.

	Pa		*A*
532	c. que mors m'a] c. morse m'as	532	c. que mors m'a ou v.] c. qu'il m'ait morse el v.
		536	va d.s.] va a d.s.
		538/9	*attributed to Robin*
		539	v. rapaisiés] v. apaisiés
534	Si te] Tant te		
540	Biau sire et je ne d.] Saciez et je n'en d.	540	(et)
542	*rubric* B	542	*rubric* LE ROI PARLE
544/6	*rubric* B		
		546	v. me d.] v. m'en d.
547	p.p. et c.] p. et p. et c.		
549	Certes j'en m.] Jou en m. tant		
550	(Tant)	550	j'en euch le m.] j'en oi la m.
		551/3	*rubric to middle of v. 553* LE ROI PARLE
		551	Hé] O
		553	P. alés] P. vien
		554/8	*rubric* LE ROI PARLE
		557	en quel l.] en quel que l., (tu)
558	di et je] di haut je		
560	quant m.a.] que m.a.		
		560/2	*these verses differ significantly and read*: Sire ce que mes amis vint/ A moi aus chans et si me tint/ Longuement bonne compaignie
		564	P. fois] P. jors
565	*third rubric* G	565	*first rubric* LE ROI

Pa

A

PARLE, *third rubric*
LE ROY

566   je t'en c.] je le c.

566   *attributed to Robin,* le
        saint D. je t'en c.] le
        cors D. je le c.
567   *rubric* LE ROI
        PARLE

568   dont demande b.]
        demande b. dont

569/72 *rubric* LE ROY
        PARLE
572   q.m.] q. m'en m.
577/8   *rubric* LE ROI

578   s. de t.] s. par t.
579/80 *attributed to Huart*

581   dous a.] biaus a.

583   p. moi vo m.] p. cha
        ma m.
586   p. caitis q.] p. hardis   586   *same*
        q.
                                        587   M.L.c.] M. ha L.c.
591   a le c.d. le t.] a sen   591   a le c.] a son c.
        c.d. se t.
                                        595   *attributed to Robin*
                                        596   *attributed to Gautier
                                                and address to
                                                Gautier is crossed out,*
                                                que v.] com v.
598   (bien), que ne v.m.]   598   que ne v.m.] qu'el ne
        qu'ele ne v.m.   v.m.
                                        601/5   *attributed to Huart*
603   com tu] que tu   603   Marotain] Marion
604   Certes] Sachez   604   *same*
605   p. se G] p. le se G.
606   Jou l'otri] Il m'est
        bel

                                        606/7   *these verses differ
                                                significantly and*

Pa | A

read: GAUTIER: Il m'est bel et je l'otroie/ Je le veill bien pren le donc/ ROBIN: Ce est tout mien

607 Cha e.] En e.
608 *attributed to Huart*

608 *attributed to Gautier*
611/2 *attributed to Marion*
613 n'en sai n.] n'en ai n.
614 Qui j.] Que j.

615 a. si p.] a. voire p.

615 *same, attributed to Huart*

616 l'osoies assaier] l'avoies assaiét

616 *omitted*

617 Ba c.] A c.

617 *same, second rubric* HUART

618 *omitted*

620 ou m.] el m.

620 *same*
621/32 *attributed to Huart to middle of v. 632*
621 Mais j'ai] Si ai
622 et herche et] charrete et
626/7 *reversed*
635 *omitted*

636 (tost)
637 (en)
639 *attributed to Peronnele*, (chi)
640/1 *attributed to Baudon*

636 S'en] Bien en
637 ne me v.] ne le v.
639 *attributed to Gautier*, boches] botes

641 *attributed to Gautier*

643 d'ui m.] du m.
644/5 *reversed*

645 *omitted*
647 *no rubric*, (Et), q. veut] Q. eüst
648 *first rubric*

	Pa		*A*
			MAROTE
649	Et jou ai] Et qui veut	649	*attributed to Huart*
		650	*first rubric* MAROT, *second rubric* HUART
651	Di de q.s. il] De q.s. il di	651	*attributed to Baudon*
652	par t.] pour t.	652	*same, attributed to Marion*
653	je p.] je des p.	653	*same*
		655	Di me d.] Or di d.
		656	*omitted*
		657	J'ai e.] E. ai je
		658	Q. n'est mie de lasté] Q. est de coulon tubé
663	(plus)	663	p. de mi] p. or di
664	jou te di] je de ti	664	O. en non Dieu] O. certes
665	j. ai] j. ai voir	665	Que jou ai] Qu'encor ai je
666	g. et c.c.] g. et c. le c.	666	Q. a gros et cras c.] Q. est cras seur le c.
		673	Et vous] Et si
675	f.o.] f. grant o.		
		680	r. maintenant] r. tout errant
685	T. veés le c. tout p.] T. vés le c. trestout p.	685	T. veés le c.] T. et vés le c.
686	*first* (le) *omitted*	686	*same*
		687/8	*attributed to Marion*
		692	Q. te s.e. il bons c.] Q. t'en s.e. il grans c.
694	f. vo g.] f. a ton g.	694	*same*
695	*attributed to Baudon,* Awar] Bawa	695	*attributed to Perrete,* Awar] Esgar
696	*first rubric* P, *second rubric* B	696	*first rubric* MAROT, *second rubric* PERRETE

	Pa		*A*
697	*attributed to Baudon,* (la), .ii. c.] .ii. grans c.	697	*attributed to Perrete,* *same*
698	*attributed to Perrete*	698	*attributed to Marion*
		702	q. tu ne] q. tu pas ne, (en)
		704	Q. je p. a c.] Q. j'ai p. en c.
705	e. con b.] e. que b.	705	Tien e. con b.] Suer e. quel b.
708	V. bele a.] V. douce a.	708	*same*
		709	*omitted*
710	m. biaus a.] m. mes a.		
715	d. trop b.] de tres b.		
716	B.e.q.] E.B.q.		
		717	vo main] vos mains
718	Et n'e.c.] En e.c.	718	*same*
		722	tenés c.] soiés c.
724	entendés] entendons	724	*same*
727	*first rubric* R	727	*first rubric* ROBIN
728	R a i m b e r g e] Haimberghe		
731	V. estes uns] V. cantés k'uns	731	V. estes uns] V. chantez com
732	En m.] A m.	732	*manuscript torn and verse unreadable to* gabe cis sos
		733	*m a n u s c r i p t unreadable to* aus mos
		734	bonne c.] bele c.
735	*first rubric* M	735	*s e c o n d r u b r i c* MAROT
		736/8	*attributed to Marion*
		739	o. tost c.] o. ains c.
		741	que tu] com tu
745	(nous)		
		746	d. qui b.] d. car b.

Pa		A	
749	con c'e. b. baler] que c'e. b. alé	749	R. con c'e.] R. que c'e.
		750	*verse omitted except* Marotele
		751/2	*attributed to Robin*
752	b. baler] b. aler, *this verse appears only as the signature for the next quire which is missing*		
		759/60	*attributed to Marion*
		759	b. alé] b. passé
		760	Tu dois de tous] De trestous dois
		760/1	*between these verses is added*: Par amors mainne nous au bos

Explicit de Robin et de Marion

APPENDICES

LI JUS DU PELERIN

LI PELERINS:

Or pais, or pais, segnieur, et a moi entendés.
Nouveles vous dirai s'un petit atendés,
Par coi trestous li pires de vous iert amendés.
Or vous taisiés tout coi, si ne me reprendés. 4

Segnieur, pelerins sui, si ai alé maint pas
Par viles, par castiaus, par chités, par trespas.
S'aroie bien mestier que je fusse a repas,
Car n'ai mie par tout mout bien trouvé mes pas. 8

Bien a trente et chienc[1] ans que je n'ai aresté,
S'ai puis en maint bon lieu et a maint saint esté.
S'ai esté au Sec Arbre et dusc'a Duresté;
Dieu grasci qui m'en a sens et pooir presté. 12

Si fui en Famenie, en Surie et en Tir;
S'alai en un païs ou on est si entir
Que on i muert errant quant on i veut mentir,
Et si est tout quemun.

LI VILAINS:

Je t'en voeil desmentir, 16

Car entendant nous fais vessie pour lanterne.
Vous ariés ja plus chier a sir en le taverne
Que aler au moustier.

LI PELERINS:

Pechié fait qui me ferne,
Car je sui mout lassés; esté ai a Luserne, 20

THE PILGRIM'S PLAY

THE PILGRIM:
Peace, peace, my lords, and listen to me.
If you wait a moment, I will tell you news
By which the worst of you will be improved.
Now be very quiet and don't blame me.   4

My lords, I am a pilgrim, and I have gone many a mile
By way of towns, castles, cities and passages.
And I would really need to be invited to eat,
For I've not found meals easily everywhere I've gone. 8

In the good thirty-five years that I haven't ceased
                                        [traveling,
I've seen many saints in many good places.
I've been to the four corners of the earth;[2]
God be thanked, who granted me the mind and strength
                                        [for it. 12

I have been to Famenie,[3] to Syria and to Tyre;
And I went to a country where people are so honest
That one dies on the spot if one tries to lie,
And everything is communal.

THE CHURL:
                        I'm going to refute what you say,   16

For you'd make us believe the moon is made of green
                                        [cheese.
You would much rather sit in the tavern
Than go to church.

THE PILGRIM:
                        He sins who censures me,
For I am very tired; I have been to Luiserne,[4]   20

129

En terre de Labour, en Toskane, en Sezile;
Par Puille m'en reving ou on tint maint concille
D'un clerc net et soustieu, gracieus et nobile,
Et le nomper du mont; nés fu de ceste ville.   24

Maistres Adans li Bochus estoit chi apelés,
Et la, Adans d'Arras.

LI VILAINS:
                              Tres mal atrouvelés
Soiiés sire! Con vous avés vos aus pelés!
Est il pour truander tres bien atripelés?   28

Alés vous en de chi, mauvais vilains puans!
Car je sai de chertain que vous estes truans.
Or tost fuiés vous ent! Ne soiés deluans,
Ou vous le comperrés!

LI PELERINS:
                              Trop par estes muans.   32

Or atendés un peu que j'aie fait mon conte.
Or pais, pour Dieu, signeur! Chis clers don je vous conte
Ert amés et prisiés et honnerés dou conte
D'Artois, si vous dirai mout bien de quel aconte.   36

Chieus maistre Adam savoit dis et chans controuver,
Et li quens desirroit un tel home a trouver.
Quant acointiés en fu, si li ala rouver
Que il feïst uns dis pour son sens esprouver.   40

Maistre Adans, qui en seut tres bien a chief venir,
En fist un dont il doit mout tres bien sousvenir,
Car biaus est a oïr et bons a retenir;
Li quoins n'en vaurroit mie .v. chens livres tenir.   44

To the land of Labeur,[5] to Toscany, to Sicily;
I returned by way of Pouille where many discussions
[ensued
About a cleric both pure and shrewd, gracious and noble,
Without equal in the world; and he was born in this
[city. 24

Master Adam the Hunchback he was called here,
And there, Adam of Arras.

THE CHURL:
                              You are completely
Unwelcome, sir! What falderol you're spouting![6]
Isn't he rather big-bellied for begging?   28

Get out of here, you miserable stinking wretch!
For I know for certain that you are a tramp.
Now flee, quick! Don't tarry,
Or you will pay for it!

THE PILGRIM:
                              You are too restless.   32
Now wait a bit till I have told my story.
Peace, for God's sake, my lords! This cleric I was telling
[you about
Was loved and prized and honored by the Count of
Artois, and I shall tell you by what account.   36

This Master Adam knew how to compose tales and songs,
And the count desired to find such a man.
When he was acquainted with him, he went to him to
[request
That he write a tale to prove his wit.   40

Master Adam, who knew well how to accomplish it,
Wrote him one well worth remembering,
For it is pleasant to hear and good to retain;
The count wouldn't prefer five hundred books to this
[one. 44

Or est mors maistre Adans, Diex li fache merchi!
A se tomble ai esté, don Jhesucrist merchi.
Li quoins le me moustra, le soie grant merchi,
Quant jou i fui l'autre an.

LI VILAINS:

Vilains, fuiés de chi!   48

Ou vous serés mout tost loussiés et desvestus.
A l'ostel serés ja autrement revestus.

LI PELERINS:
Et comment vous nomme on, qui si estes testus?

LI VILAINS:
Comment, sire vilains? Gautelos li Testus.   52

LI PELERINS:
Or veilliés un petit, biaus dous amis, atendre,
Car on m'a fait mout lonc de ceste vile entendre
Qu'ens en l'onnour du clerc que Dieus a volut prendre,
Doit on dire ses dis chi endroit et aprendre.   56

Si sui pour che chi enbatus.

GAUTIERS:
Fuiés ou vous serés batus,
Que diable vous ont raporté.
Trop vous ai ore deporté,   60
Que je ne vous ai embrunkiet
Ne[7] que cist saint sont enfunkiet
Il ont veü maint roy en France.

LI PELERINS:
Hé, vrais Dieus, envoiés souffrance   64
Tous cheus qui me font desraison.

GUIOS:
Warnet, as tu le raison

Now Master Adam is dead, may God have mercy on him!
I have been to his grave, for which I thank Jesus Christ.
The count, by his grace, showed it to me
When I was there the other year.

THE CHURL:

Wretch, get out of here!   48

Or you will soon be beat up and stripped.
At the inn you'll be arrayed in another manner.

THE PILGRIM:
What's your name, you who are so headstrong?

THE CHURL:
My name, Sir Wretch? Gautier Bighead.   52

THE PILGRIM:
Be pleased then, my friend, to forebear a bit longer,
For far away from this city I was made to understand
That here, in honor of the cleric whom God has taken
                                                        [away,
One must tell his tales and learn them in this place.   56

For that reason I have shown up here.

GAUTIER:
Flee or you will be beaten up,
For devils have brought you.
Too long now have I borne with you   60
Without having trounced you in the mud
Like those blackened saints
Who have seen many a king of France.[8]

THE PILGRIM:
Oh, true God, send suffering   64
To all those who do me wrong.

GUIOT:
Garnier, have you been listening to

Oïe de cest païsant,
Et comment il nous va disant   68
Ses bourdes dont il nous abuffe?

WARNÉS:
Oiie, donne li une buffe.
Je sai bien que c'est .i. mais hom.

GUIOS:
Tenés! Ore alés en maison!   72
Et si n'i venés plus, vilains!

ROGAUS:
Que c'est? Mesires sains Guillains,
Warnier, vous puist faire baler!
Pour coi en faites vous aler   76
Chest home qui riens ne vous grieve?

WARNERS:
Rogaut, a poi que je ne crieve,
Tant fort m'anuie se parole.

ROGAUS:
Taisiés vous, Warnier! Il parole   80
De maistre Adan, le clerc d'onneur,
Le joli, le largue donneur,
Qui ert de toutes vertus plains.
De tout le mont doit estre plains,   84
Car mainte bele grace avoit,
Et seur tous biau diter savoit,
Et s'estoit parfais en chanter.

WARNIERS:
Savoit il dont gent enchanter?   88
Or pris je trop mains son affaire.

ROGAUS:
Nenil, ains savoit canchons faire,
Partures et motés entés.
De che fist il a grant plentés,   92

This peasant's discourse,
And how he goes on telling us   68
His fibs with which he fools us?

GARNIER:
  Yes, give him a smack.
  I know for sure he's an evil man.

GUIOT:
  Here! Now go home!   72
  And don't ever come back, you wretch!

ROGER:
  What's this? May the Honorable Saint Guy,
  Garnier, make you dance![9]
  Why are you chasing away   76
  This man who does nothing to harm you?

GARNIER:
  Roger, I almost died,
  His talking annoyed me so.

ROGER:
  Be quiet, Garnier! He speaks   80
  About Master Adam, the honorable cleric,
  The handsome, the generous giver,
  Who was full of all virtues.
  He should be mourned by everyone,   84
  For he had many lovely qualities,
  And knew better than anyone how to tell a good tale,
  And was perfect in singing.

GARNIER:
  So he knew how to bewitch people?[10]   88
  Now I value his character even less.

ROGER:
  No, it was songs that he wrote,
  Short poems and entire motets.
  He wrote plenty of those,   92

Et balades je ne sai quantés.

WARNIERS:
Je te pri dont que tu m'en cantés
Une qui soit auques commune.

ROGAUS:
Volontiers voir, jou en sai une   96
Qu'il fist que je te canterai.

WARNIERS:
Or di et je t'escouterai,
Et tous nos estris abatons.

ROGAUS:
Il n'est si bonne viande que matons.   100
Est ceste bonne, Warnier, frere?

WARNIERS:
Ele est l'estronc de vostre mere!
Doit on tele canchon prisier?
Par le cul Dieu! J'en apris ier   104
Une qui en vaut les quarante.

ROGAUS:
Par amours, Warnier, or le cante.

WARNIERS:
Volentiers, foi que doi m'amie:
Se je n'i aloie, je n'iroie mie.   108
De tel chant se doit on vanter!

ROGAUS:
Par foi, il t'avient a chanter
Aussi bien qu'il fait tumer l'ours!

WARNIERS:
Mais c'estes vous qui estes lours;   112
Uns grans caitis loufe-se-waigne!

And I don't know how many ballads.

GARNIER:
Please, then, sing me one of them
That is somewhat known.

ROGER:
Most gladly, I know one   96
That he wrote that I'll sing for you.

GARNIER:
Say it then and I'll listen to you,
And we'll forget all our disputes.

ROGER:
There is no finer food than curdled milk.   100
Isn't that good, brother Garnier?

GARNIER:
It's your mother's turd!
Must one prize such drivel?
Zounds! I learned one yesterday   104
That's worth forty of those.

ROGER:
Please, Garnier, sing it.

GARNIER:
Willingly, by the faith I owe my sweetheart:
If I weren't going there, I wouldn't go.   108
That's a song to brag about!

ROGER:
By my faith, singing fits you
Like it fits a bear to dance!

GARNIER:
No, it's you who are the numskull;   112
A big ole miserable glutton!

ROGAUS:

    Par foi, or ai je grant engaigne
    De vo grande melancolie.
    Je feroie hui mais grant folie   116
    Se je men sens metoie au vostre.
    Biaus preudons, mes consaus vous loe
    Que chi ne faites plus de noise.

LI PELERINS:

    Loés vous dont que je m'en voise?   120

ROGAUS:

    Oïl, voir.

LI PELERINS:

              Et je m'en irai.
    Ne plus parole n'i dirai,
    Car je n'ai mestier c'on me fiere.

GUIOS:

    Hé, Diex, je ne mengai puis tierche,   124
    Et s'est ja plus nonne de jour;
    Et si ne puis avoir sejour
    Se je ne boi ou dorc ou masque.
    Je m'en vois; j'ai faite me tasque,   128
    Ne je n'ai chi plus riens que faire.

ROGAUS:

    Warnet.

WARNIERS:

          Que?

ROGAUS:

               Veus tu bien faire?
    Alons vers Aiieste a le foire.

WARNÉS:

    Soit, mais anchois voeil aler boire.   132
    Mau dehais ait qui n'i venra!

ROGER:
In faith, now I really am vexed
With your bad humor.
From now on I'd be crazy 116
To come down to your level.
My good fellow, my advice to you is
Not to make any more of a disturbance here.

THE PILGRIM:
Do you advise me then to go away? 120

ROGER:
Indeed I do.

THE PILGRIM:
                    Then I'll leave.
Not another word will I say here,
For I have no need to be struck.

GUIOT:
My God, I haven't eaten since nine o'clock, 124
And three o'clock has already passed;
And I can have no rest
If I do not drink or sleep or eat.
I'm leaving; I have done my task, 128
And I have nothing left to do here.

ROGER:
Garnier.

GARNIER:
                    What?

ROGER:
                    What about this?
Let's go to Ayette to the fair.

GARNIER:
All right, but first I want to go drinking. 132
A curse on anyone who won't come along!

NOTES

1. *Chieuc* in manuscript.

2. *Sec arbre* and *Duresté* are legendary place names which symbolize the far reaches of the world. See Dufournet ed. 176.

3. A legendary country. See Dufournet ed. 176.

4. Saracen city destroyed by Charlemagne. See Dufournet ed. 177.

5. In southern Italy. See Dufournet ed. 177.

6. Literally "How you have peeled your garlic!" See Dufournet ed. 177.

7. *Ue* in manuscript.

8. The meaning here is obscure. Is the image one of saints' relics blackened by time, statues of saints darkened with age, or perhaps saints blackened by martyrdom at the stake? See Dufournet ed. 178 for a discussion of the words *embrunkiet* and *enfunkiet*.

9. Allusion to the dance of Saint Guy. See Dufournet ed. 178.

10. Garnier understands *en chanter* as *enchanteor* ("sorcerer"). See Dufournet ed. 178.

INTERPOLATION #1
(between vv. 680 & 681)

WARNIERS:
Robin, ou vas tu?

ROBINS:

          A Bailues
Chi devant, pour de la viande,
Car l'aval a feste trop grande.
Venras tu avoec nous mengier?   4

WARNIERS:
On en feroit, je cuit, dangier.

ROBINS:
Non feroit nient.

WARNIERS:

          Jou irai donques.

GUIOS:
Rogiaut!

ROGAUS:

    Que?

GUIOS:

          Or ne veïstes onques
Plus grant deduit ne plus grant feste   8
Que j'ai veü.

ROGAUS:

          Ou?

INTERPOLATION #1
(between vv. 680 & 681)

GARNIER:
Robin, where are you going?

ROBIN:
                              To Bailleul
A little way from here, for some food,
For down that way, there's a great party going on.
Will you come eat with us?   4

GARNIER:
I think someone would object.

ROBIN:
No, nobody would.

GARNIER:
                    Then I'll come.

GUIOT:
Roger!

ROGER:
          What?

GUIOT:
                    You have never seen
More fun or better festivities   8
Than I just saw.

ROGER:
          Where?

GUIOS:

Vers Aiieste.
Par tans nouveles en aras.
Veü i ai trop biaus baras.

ROGAUS:
Et de cui?

GUIOS:

Tous de pastouriaus.   12
Acaté i ai ches bourriaus
Avoecques m'amie Saret.

ROGAUS:
Guiot, or alons vir Maret
L'aval; s'i trouverons Wautier,   16
Car j'oï dire qu'il vaut[1] ier
Peronnele, te sereur, prendre,
Et ele n'i vaut pas entendre
Si en eüst parlé a ti.   20

GUIOS:
Point ne l'ara, car il bati
L'autre semaine .i. mien neveu,
Et je jurai et fis le veu
Que il seroit aussi bastus.   24

ROGAUS:
Guiot, tous sera abatus
Chis estris, se tu me veus croire,
Car Gautiers te[2] donra a boire
A genous par amendement.   28

GUIOS:
Je le voeil bien si faitement,
Puis que vous vous i assentés.
Vés chi .ii. bons cornés, sentés,
Que j'ai acatés a le foire.   32

GUIOT:
                                                 Near Ayette.
    You'll hear about it soon.
    I saw some wonderful entertainment there.

ROGER:
    By whom?

GUIOT:
                                  All by shepherds.   12
    I bought these headdresses there
    With my sweetheart Sarette.

ROGER:
    Guiot, let's go see Marion
    Down that way; we'll find Gautier there,   16
    For I heard it said that yesterday he wanted
    To marry your sister, Peronnelle,
    And she didn't want to hear anything of it
    Without having spoken to you about it.   20

GUIOT:
    He'll never have her, for he beat up
    A nephew of mine the other week,
    And I swore and vowed
    That he would likewise get a beating.   24

ROGER:
    Guiot, this whole dispute
    Will be settled, believe me,
    For Gautier will offer you a drink
    On his knees to make up.   28

GUIOT:
    I am willing in that case,
    Since you two have agreed on it.
    Here are two good horns, look,
    That I bought at the fair.   32

ROGAUS:
Guiot, vent m'en .i., a tout boire.

GUIOS:
En non Dieu, Rogaut, non ferai,
Mais le meilleur vous presterai.
Prendés le quel que vous volés.   36

ROGAUS:
Awar! Que chis vient adolés
Et qu'il vient petite aleüre!

GUIOS:
C'est Warnerés de le Couture.
Est il sotement escourchiés!   40

WARNIERS:
Segneur, je sui trop courechiés.

GUIOS:
Comment?

WARNIERS:
               Mehalés est agute,
M'amie, et s'a esté dechute,
Car on dist que ch'est de no prestre.   44

ROGAUS:
En non Dieu, Warnier, bien puet estre,
Car ele i aloit trop souvent.

WARNIERS:
Hé! Las! Jou avoie en couvent
De li temprement espouser.   48

GUIOS:
Tu te pues bien trop dolouser,
Biaus tres dous amis; ne te caille,
Car ja ne meteras maaille,

ROGER:
Guiot, sell me one, for repayment in drink.

GUIOT:
In God's name, Roger, I won't,
But I'll lend you the better one.
Take whichever one you like. 36

ROGER:
Hey, look! How sadly and slowly
That person is coming this way!

GUIOT:
Why, it's Garnier from Couture.
Isn't he ridiculously trussed up! 40

GARNIER:
My lords, I am quite angry.

GUIOT:
What's wrong?

GARNIER:
Mehalet, my sweetheart,
Is pregnant, and she was seduced,
For they say that it was our priest. 44

ROGER:
In God's name, Garnier, that could be,
For she used to go there quite often.

GARNIER:
Alas! I had promised
To marry her soon. 48

GUIOT:
You have good reason to be upset,
My very dear friend; but don't worry,
For you will never spend a penny,

Que bien sai, a l'enfant warder.   52

ROGAUS:
A che doit on bien resvarder,
Foi que je doi Sainte Marie.

WARNIERS:
Certes, segnieur, vo compaignie
Me fait metre jus men anoi.   56

GUIOS:
Or faisons un peu d'esbanoi
Entreus que nous atenderons
Robin.

WARNIERS:
          En non Dieu, non ferons,
Car il vient chi les grans walos.   60

ROBINS:
Warnet, tu ne sés? Mehalos
Est hui agute de no prestre!

WARNIERS:
Hé! Tout li diale i puissent estre,
Robert, comme avés maise geule!   64

ROBINS:
Toudis a ele esté trop veule,
Warnier, si m'aït Diex, et sote.

ROGAUS:
Robert, foi que devés Marote,
Metés ceste cose en delui!   68

ROBINS:
Je n'i parlerai plus de lui.
Alons ent.

    I warrant, to take care of the child.   52

ROGER:
    One really has to watch out for that,
    By my faith in Holy Mary.

GARNIER:
    Your company, my lords, has certainly
    Helped me chase away my torment.   56

GUIOT:
    And now, let's enjoy ourselves
    While we wait for
    Robin.

GARNIER:
          In God's name, we won't need to,
    For here he comes at full gallop!   60

ROBIN:
    Garnier, don't you know? Mehalet
    Is pregnant now by our priest!

GARNIER:
    Hey! By all the meddling devils,
    Robin, you have a dirty mouth!   64

ROBIN:
    She always was fickle,
    Garnier, so help me God, and foolish.

ROGER:
    Robin, by all your faith in Marion,
    Put off discussion of this matter!   68

ROBIN:
    I won't speak anymore of it.
    Let's go.

WARNIERS:
> Alons.

ROGAUS:
> Passe avant.

INTERPOLATION #2
(between vv. 706 & 707)

(ROBINS):
Or faisons tost feste de nous.

ROGAUS:
Wautier, or te met a genous
Devant Guiot premierement,
Et si li fai amendement   4
De chou que sen neveu batis,
Car il s'estoit ore aätis
Que il te feroit a sousfrir.

GAUTIERS:
Volés que je li voise offrir   8
A boire?

ROGAUS:
> Oïl.

GAUTIERS:
> Guiot, buvés!

GUIOS:
Gautier, levés vous sus, levés!
Je vous pardoins tout le meffait
C'a mi ni as miens avés fait,   12
Et voeil que nous soions ami.

GARNIER:

Yes, let's.

ROGER:

You go ahead.

INTERPOLATION #2
(between vv. 706 & 707)

(ROBIN):

Now let's start enjoying ourselves.

ROGER:

But first, Gautier, down on your knees
In front of Guiot,
And make amends to him   4
For having beat up his nephew,
Because he was just now vowing
That he would make you suffer for it.

GAUTIER:

Do you want me to offer him   8
A drink?

ROGER:

Yes.

GAUTIER:

Guiot, drink!

GUIOT:

Gautier, stand up, come on!
I forgive you for all the wrong
You have done to me or mine,   12
And I want us to be friends.

PERONNELE:
Guyot, frere, parole a mi.
Viens te cha sir, si te repose.
Que m'aportes tu?

GUIOS:
                    Nule cose,   16
Mais t'aras bel jouel demain.

MARIONS:
Robin, dous amis, cha, te main.

PERONNELLE:
Guiot, my brother, come talk to me.
Come sit here, and rest.
What have you brought me?

GUIOT:
                                        Nothing,   16
But you will have a pretty bauble tomorrow.

MARION:
Robin, sweetheart, give me your hand.

NOTES

1. *Vant* in manuscript.

2. *De* in manuscript.

GARLAND LIBRARY OF MEDIEVAL LITERATURE

JAMES J. WILHELM
AND LOWRY NELSON, JR.
General Editors

Series A (Texts and Translations)
Series B (Translations Only)

GUILLAUME DE MACHAUT
The Fountain of Love (La Fonteinne Amoureuse), and Two Other Love Vision Poems
Edited and translated by
R. Barton Palmer
Series A

DER STRICKER
Daniel of the Blossoming Valley
Translated by Michael Resler
Series B

THE MARVELS OF RIGOMER
Translated by Thomas E. Vesce
Series B

CHRÉTIEN DE TROYES
The Story of the Grail (Li Contes del Graal), or *Perceval*
Edited by Rupert T. Pickens and translated by William W. Kibler
Series A

HELDRIS DE CORNUÄLLE
The Story of Silence (Le Roman de Silence)
Translated by Regina Psaki
Series B

ROMANCES OF ALEXANDER
Translated by Dennis M. Kratz
Series B

THE CAMBRIDGE SONGS
(CARMINA CANTABRIGIENSA)
Edited and translated by
Jan M. Ziolkowski
Series A

GUILLAUME DE MACHAUT
Le Confort d'Ami (Comfort for a Friend)
Edited and translated by
R. Barton Palmer
Series A

CHRISTINE DE PIZAN
Christine's Vision
Translated by Glenda K. McLeod
Series B

MORIZ VON CRAÛN
Edited and translated by
Stephanie Cain Van D'Elden
Series A

THE ACTS OF ANDREW IN THE COUNTRY OF THE CANNIBALS
Translated by Robert Boenig
Series B

RAZOS AND TROUBADOUR SONGS
Translated by William E. Burgwinkle
Series B

MECHTHILD VON MAGDEBURG
Flowing Light of the Divinity
Translated by Christiane Mesch Galvani; edited, with an introduction, by Susan Clark
Series B

ROBERT DE BORON
The Grail Trilogy
Translated by George Diller
Series B

TILL EULENSPIEGEL
His Adventures
Translated, with introduction and notes, by Paul Oppenheimer
Series B

FRANCESCO PETRARCH
Rime Disperse
Edited and translated by Joseph Barber
Series A

GUILLAUME DE DEGUILEVILLE
The Pilgrimage of Human Life (Le Pèlerinage de la vie humaine)
Translated by Eugene Clasby
Series B

RENAUT DE BÂGÉ
Le Bel Inconnu (Li Biaus Descouneüs; The Fair Unknown)
Edited by Karen Fresco; translated by Colleen P. Donagher; music edited by Margaret P. Hasselman
Series A

THOMAS OF BRITAIN
Tristran
Edited and translated by Stewart Gregory
Series A

KUDRUN
Translated by Marion E. Gibbs and Sidney M. Johnson
Series B

PENNINC AND PIETER VOSTAERT
Roman van Walewein
Edited and translated by David F. Johnson
Series A

MEDIEVAL LITERATURE OF POLAND
An Anthology
Translated by Michael J. Mikoś
Series B

HELYAS OR LOHENGRIN
Late Medieval Transformations of the Swan Knight Legend
Edited and translated by
Salvatore Calomino
Series A